The Game is Up

Book 1

We believe that the Bible is God's word to mankind, and that it contains everything we need to know in order to be reconciled with God and live in a way that is pleasing to him. Therefore, we believe it is vital to teach children accurately from the Bible, being careful to teach each passage's true meaning in an appropriate way for childlren, rather than selecting a 'children's message' from a Biblical passage.

Contributors

Trevor Blundell
Thalia Blundell
John & Carolyn Chamberlain
Annie Gemmill
Steve Johnson
Guy Lachlan
Nick Margesson
Leonie Mason
Kirsteen McCulloch
Kathy Pierce

Published by Christian Focus Publications Ltd. Geanies House, Fearn, Tain, Ross-shire, IV20 1TW
Tel: 01862 871 011 Fax: 01862 871 699

Cover design by Tim Charnick
Illustrations by Tim Charnick
Printed by Arrowsmith

This book and other in the series can be purchased from your local Christian bookshop. Alternatively you can write to TnT Ministries direct or place your order with the publisher.

ISBN 1-85792-5505

TnT Ministries (which stands for Teaching and Training Ministries) was launched in February 1993 by Christians from a broad variety of denominational backgrounds who are concerned that teaching the Bible to children be taken seriously. The leaders were in charge of a Sunday School of 50 teachers ar St Helen's Bishopgate, an evangelical church in the city of London, for 13 years, during which time a range of Biblical teaching material has been developed. TnT Ministries also runs training days for Sunday School teachers.

Contents

Introduction

The great desire of our hearts is that children everywhere will come to love and trust Jesus as their Lord and Saviour. It is our firm belief that this happens primarily through the teaching of God's word in the Bible. This book of games and ideas is designed as a resource to complement and support Bible teaching. It has been written as a companion volume to the 'On the Way' Bible teaching programme, but is suitable for use in any situation where the Bible is being taught to children.

Teaching the Bible is an exacting task. Teaching the Bible to children is even more so. The concepts are sometimes hard to communicate and are often contrary to the norms in the secular society in which they live. They are used to an interactive style of learning and they want to have fun. Traditionally we have tended to separate off the 'Bible teaching' slot from the rest of the activities in our children's programmes which are fun but have no Bible content. How much better to make every part of the programme count in the teaching of God's word! Since children learn by repetition, why teach something once when you can teach it several times, using all the activities and games to contribute to the learning process? In this way not only is learning enhanced but the Bible is exciting, relevant and truly central to the group's activities.

In this book we have outlined three supplementary activities - the Warm Up, the Consolidation and the Wind Up. Though this is only one model of an integrated teaching approach, it has been used by TnT Ministries with great success for many years. We have found consistently that with this kind of repetition even the smallest child can learn big things about God.

Warm Up

This is a short activity or presentation designed to arrest the attention of the child and prepare them for the Bible teaching which is to follow.

Consolidation

This is a constructive game or activity designed to reinforce the key concepts, theme, aim or details of the Bible story that has just been taught. It generally involves plenty of physical activity and some simple equipment.

Wind Up

A Wind Up is the final summation of the days teaching. It involves linking the Warm Up, the Bible story and the Consolidation together, emphasising the central teaching point.

Warm Ups and Wind Ups take around 5 minutes and a Consolidation game 10-15 minutes. For each Bible story there are 2 schemes of Warm Ups, Consolidations and Wind Ups described. One will often require more space or more equipment.

The ideas and suggestions in this book are only guidelines for you to adapt and change in line with the age, number and needs of your children and limitations of your meeting space. We would stress that they should be used alongside, not in place of, teaching directly from the Bible.

In some Warm Ups the leader demonstrates negative qualities, such as favouritism. When acting out of character we suggest that you don a hat or jacket, or call yourself a different name, so that the younger children do not equate the bad points with the leader.

Creating your own Games

Why not create your own games, custom made to serve your children, and take advantage of the special possibilities of your meeting place? It's easy if you take account of a few basic principles.

The first task is to spend time in the Bible. Your game is a teaching opportunity and you need to understand the message of your passage for the day before you will know the concept, aim or details you want to teach from it via the game. There are four important elements to designing and running successful games.

Rules

There need to be SIMPLE RULES which are easily understood and which can be enforced to make the game fun, safe, workable and educational.

- Explain the rules, then ask questions to see if they have understood them. Then ask if they have any questions before repeating the rules and starting the game. This may sound laborious but it is a good investment of time.
- Start the game with a clear command, e.g. 'When I say "Go"', or, 'When I drop my hand'.
- The rules must be applied consistently and rule breakers need to be dealt with firmly.

Participation

Games are for joining in, not for watching, and so good games involve lots of participation. To make a game fun for everyone, as many children as possible need to be on the move at the same time. However, a safe environment must be preserved at all times.

- Games involving cross movements of children or games depending on speed alone are best avoided.
- Small or otherwise vulnerable children must be protected. Sometimes it is possible to design a game where these children have a different role from the older ones. All children should be encouraged to take part but never forced.
- It is wise to have a strategy for stopping the game and restoring order if necessary. The command 'Statues' or 'Freeze' will do this. A 'Sin Bin' is also useful for rule breakers.

A Scoring System

A scoring system is needed to determine who wins. Children are naturally competitive and learning to win and lose graciously is a valuable social skill. However:

- It must be absolutely fair and administered by an impartial adult.
- It must be understandable, preferably visual.
- All efforts should be affirmed and congratulated.

A running commentary by the game leader is very helpful.

Equipment

Equipment os some sort is needed for nearly all games. Children like to hold, carry and hide things.

- Almost anything can be used in games, but it must be safe. It is unwise to include anything which might be used as a weapon.
- It should be easy to reset if necessary during the game and easy to clear up at the end.
- The ideal is to have a small store of safe, versatile itmes for use in your games.

List of suggested items

Balloons & blow-up items
Balls of string
Buckets
Cardboard boxes
Cardboard tubes
Clothes-lines x 18m. lengths
Dried peas, beans, lentils, etc.
Disposable or plastic cups

Empty plastic soft drink bottles
Newspapers
Small items to act as tokens
e.g. bottle tops, corks, buttons
Plastic jar lids
Plastic laundry baskets or sledges
Puppets - two - one boy - one girl

Sheet or parachute
Soft sponge balls
Sponges
Table tennis balls

CREATION

Text: Read and study Genesis 1:1 - 2:9,15

Teaching Point: God made everything and it was good.

WARM UP 1

The object is to teach that God made all things out of nothing. Prior to the session collect some empty containers, labelled sugar, flour, currants, etc., an empty butter dish and egg carton, a cake tin, mixing bowl, cooking implements and a box to be an oven. Dress up as a cook and tell the children that you are going to make a cake. Pretend to take out spoonfuls of ingredients and mix them into a bowl. Put the contents of the bowl into a cake tin and put into the pretend oven. Take it out quickly and show it to the children. Point out that there is nothing there and ask them why. Lead into the fact that you cannot make a cake from nothing; you need something to start from - ingredients. Say, 'Today's true story from the Bible is about someone who made something from nothing. I want you to come back after the Bible story and tell me:

1. Who made something from nothing?
2. What did he make from nothing?
3. How did he make it from nothing?'

For younger children, only questions 1 and 2 may be appropriate.

CONSOLIDATION 1

The object is to teach the order of the days of creation. Start by demonstrating each action for the children to copy. The leader will call out 'Day .... (a number between 1 and 7)'. The children will perform the appropriate action for that day, A whistle is helpful to restore order. When blown the children freeze. Repeat the process for as long as they are interested, but do not push their boredom threshold.

Actions:

1. Day and night - cover eyes with hands to make dark (night) and remove them to make light (day).
2. Sky - point to the heavens.
3. Sea & land - run to the water's edge and retreat as the waters come up the beach.
4. Sun, moon & stars - open and close hands to show twinkling stars.
5. Fish & birds - open mouths wide and close them for the fish, flap arms up and down for birds.
6. Animals and people - make animal sounds or just talk.
7. Rest - fall onto floor and stay motionless.

An alternative way is for the leader to say, 'Let there be light, etc.' and to do the appropriate action. Whenever the leader prefaces the statement with the words, 'God said ...', the children copy the leader. When those words are omitted the children do nothing.

WIND UP 1

Review the questions from the Warm Up. Make sure the children understand the answers. Remind them that God started and completed everything, it was perfect and good. It was all made from nothing and God did it by speaking (i.e. commanding), which shows how powerful he is. Go over the order of creation. End by reinforcing the fact that God made everything and it was all very good.

CREATION

Text: Read and study Genesis 1:1 - 2:9,15

Teaching Point: God made everything and it was good.

WARM UP 2

The object is to teach about someone who made everything by commanding it to happen. Place some items of fruit or some toys on a table. If using fruit, choose an apple or an orange and a banana. Place the orange on the table so the children can see it. Ask for a volunteer from the children and instruct them to talk to the orange and change it into a banana or an apple without touching it. They can only use their voices to command. Nothing will happen. The leader then does the same. Nothing will happen. Substitute the other fruits and repeat the process. Ask the children why the fruit did not change. Lead them on to reply that you cannot change something or make something by speaking to it. Say, 'Today's true story from the Bible is about someone who made everything by speaking or commanding it to happen. I want you to tell me later:

1. Who spoke and made things happen?
2 What happened when he spoke?'

If you are using toys as the teaching props, command them to move or perform, especially the electronic ones, but with no touching. Lead into the story as outlined above.

CONSOLIDATION 2

The object is to teach the order of creation. Use pictures to identify the different days of creation. Place them face down on the floor at random. The children march around in a circle outside the pictures and when told to stop, choose one child to turn a picture over. When the picture is turned over, ask the group, 'Which day is this?' Do not continue until the right answer is given. Repeat until all the pictures are turned over and then place them in order of Day 1 to Day 7. Repeat the creation order as you go, e.g. Day 1 – day and night, Day 2 – Sky.

Pieces of paper with numbers 1-7 inclusive can also be used and the same rules applied. The 14 sheets of paper, 7 numbered and 7 with pictures, could be arranged at random in a circle. If the children are unable to match the number and picture, use the actions from Consolidation 1 as reinforcement, e.g. for Day 7, rest - fall on the floor and stay motionless.

WIND UP 2

Review the questions from the Warm Up. Remind the children that only God can bring things into being by his words. We cannot do that because we are not God. Everything that was created happened by God commanding it to happen. Remind them of the order of creation.

THE FALL

Text: Read and study Genesis 2:15 - 3:24

Teaching Point: Sin has consequences.

WARM UP 1

Place a box of chocolates on a table in view of the children and a sign in front which says, 'Do not touch'. On the reverse side of the sign print the words, 'We are not friends'. Explain that the chocolates are yours and you need them for a special reason. State that if the chocolates go missing, everyone will be guilty and they cannot be your friends anymore. Discuss the following: Is it good to have rules? Do you have rules at home, at school, at the group? What rules do you have? Are there rules for crossing the road? Check the chocolates are still safe. Turn over the 'Do not touch' card and read out the consequences of breaking the rules, i.e. 'We are not friends'. Say, 'In today's true story from the Bible we will learn about a rule that was broken. I want you to come back and tell me:

1. Who made the rule?
2. Who broke the rule?
3. What rule was broken?
4. What were the consequences/results?'

CONSOLIDATION 1

Organise the children into teams for a relay race or to run an obstacle course. Place the table with the chocolates from the Warm Up at the side of the games area. *Ideas for relay races: Run to a point and return; Hop to a point and return; Skip to a point and return; Jump like a frog; Walk while holding ankles.*

Explain the rules and conduct the races. While the children are concentrating on the races, a leader secretly removes the chocolates. At the conclusion of the races, call for the table to be brought forward and discover that the chocolates are missing. Turn the 'Do not touch' sign around so that 'We are not friends' is visible. Try to find the thief and when you cannot, tell the children that you cannot be friends anymore. Place a partition, sheet or safe barrier between the leader and children. Any further messages will need to be passed back and forth through a small opening in the barrier. A different leader should do the Wind Up. If there is insufficient space for a relay race or obstacle course, organise a passive activity that will hold the attention of the children while someone removes the chocolates.

Simple team games could include:

1. Building the tallest tower from paper cups.
2. Table football with a table tennis ball, flicking with fingers or blowing.
3. Spin the bottle using an empty plastic soft drink container, the neck pointing to the person who is out.
4. Assemble the newspaper. Get three or four different newspapers (or same newspapers, but different days). Mix the pages up and reassemble into one complete paper.

WIND UP 1

Review the four questions from the Warm Up. Remind the children that when Adam and Eve disobeyed God's rules they were punished, because it spoilt the special relationship they had with God. God had told them what would happen if they disobeyed him and he always keeps his word. Remind them of what happened when someone stole the chocolates. Point out that the barrier between the leader and children is a picture of the barrier sin puts between God and mankind. End by stating that Jesus died to take that barrier away, so we can be friends with God.

THE FALL

Text: Read and study Genesis 2:15 - 3:24

Teaching Point: Sin has consequences.

WARM UP 2

Leader 1 brings out a cake, precut in slices, and places it on a table. Leader 2 wants a piece. Leader 1 says no, the cake is for later. Leader 1 goes off to do something else, leaving Leader 2 reading the newspaper. Leader 2 looks at the cake. What a delicious looking cake, etc. Leader 2 picks up the plate. Will Leader 1 notice if I just have a bit? Eventually, Leader 2 takes a slice, eats a bit from the middle and replaces the slice. No-one will notice. Leader 1 returns and discovers that a bit of cake has been eaten. Leader 2 gets sent out with no cake.

Say, 'Today's true story from the Bible is about people who did something they were told not to. I want to know:

1. Who were the people?
2. What did they do wrong?
3. What were the consequences?'

CONSOLIDATION 2

Place sheets of newspaper or carpet squares randomly on the floor, to be stepping stones. Do not put anything on a slippery wooden floor that will move when the children walk on it. When you call out, 'Stepping stones', the children have to walk only on the stepping stones. When you call out, 'River', they walk on anything but the stepping stones. Make a course to go from A to B and back again. Only one person is allowed on a stepping stone at a time. On the command, 'Statues', the children must remain motionless. The last person to arrive is eliminated from the game,as are those who break the rules. Repeat as often as required.

If space is limited you could play the touch game. Place objects on or around the table or room, e.g. football, cushion, newspaper, shoes, etc. Call out an item and the children have to run and touch the object as fast as possible. The last one to do so is out. Continue until only one person is left. You can use the floor, chairs and wall.

WIND UP 2

Review the questions from the Warm Up. Remind the children that sin (disobedience) spoilt the relationship between God and Adam and Eve. God's rules were given to maximise the relationships between him and his people. The rules were good but the disobedience did eternal damage to all relationships. Point out that, when we play games, if we do not keep the rules we do not have a nice time and the game is spoilt.

THE FLOOD

Text: Read and study Genesis 6:5 - 8:22; 9:8-17.

Teaching Point: God punishes sin but provides an escape route for those who trust him.

WARM UP 1

If you have a large area or you are near to a football field you could measure out the dimensions of the ark. Do not tell the children what you are measuring. 'I want you to help me measure something and when we have measured it, can you guess what it could be?' Rope, string or plastic clothes-lines can be used as they come in 18 metre lengths and the children will love stretching them out and joining them up. The measurements of the ark were 136 metres long and 23 metres wide. Use four household buckets to place at each corner of the rectangle. Leave the rope/clothes-lines lying on the ground so that the children can easily visualise the size. If you do not have enough space show the children how far down the road from the church 136 metres goes and how wide 23 metres is. Once you have shown the children tell them that the thing you are measuring was also 14 metres high. Today's true story from the Bible is about something this big (point to the boundary markers). What could it be? After the Bible story come back and tell me what was so big and what it was used for. If the area is not large enough to measure the full dimensions of the ark, try and measure your area and relate it to the size of the ark, e.g. three times, six times as big as this building.

CONSOLIDATION 1

The object of this game is to collect the animals two by two and place them in the ark. If you have space, mark out a rectangular area with masking tape or buckets to represent a miniature ark. Gather pictures of animals, birds and reptiles to place in the ark (do two photocopies of them as large as possible). Place these face down on the floor, randomly surrounding the ark. On the command, 'Go!' the children pick up a picture and try to find its copy. Once found, put the pair into the ark. Continue until all animals are in the ark. You need two to three pairs of animals for each child.

For restricted space, use the same approach as above but use smaller photocopies. A nominated child is asked to turn one picture over and then asked to find its matching partner. If the second picture does not match, both pictures are turned face down and another child chosen to turn up a picture and find its match. Repeat until all are found. To avoid discouragement and speed up the game, the children could be allowed to turn three pictures to find a matching a pair. When the pair is found everyone shouts, 'Into the ark'. Place the pictures face up in the ark.

WIND UP 1

Ask the children what it was that was so big. It was the ark! What was the ark for? It was to save Noah, his family and the animals from the flood. What was the flood for? To punish all the wicked people who hated God and one another. Only Noah loved God and obeyed him, so he was saved. God made a way of escape.

THE FLOOD

Text: Read and study Genesis 6:5 – 8:22; 9:8-17

Teaching Point: God punishes sin but provides an escape route for those who trust him.

WARM UP 2

God preserves a remnant in Noah and his family. Place eight bright buttons or similar items into a packet of cereal and re-seal the top. (Instead of cereal, you can substitute shredded tissue or other absorbent paper in an empty box.) Empty the contents of the cereal box onto a table or tray and spread out thinly. The buttons should stand out as being different from all the cereal pieces. Ask for eight volunteers to pick out a button each and place them in a lightweight, buoyant container such as an empty plastic box, away from the cereal pieces. Tell the children that the eight buttons are different from all the cereal pieces. Tip the cereal pieces into a bucket of water and watch them go soggy then start to disintegrate. NB smaller children may eat the cereal, so please watch carefully. A leader should supervise. Place the container with the eight buttons into the bucket. It should float and continue to do so even when you keep pouring cupfuls of water into the bucket.

Say, 'Today's true story from the Bible is about 8 people who were kept safe. I want you to tell me:

1. Who were they?
2. Who kept them safe?
3. What were they saved from?'

CONSOLIDATION 2

The object of the game is for the eight people in the ark to feed all the animals. If possible, divide into teams of eight. Sit the children down in a line to form a chain and pass items from one person to the next until all the items are moved from the food store at the front to the animals at the back (end of the line). Who can do it the fastest? The items can be sponges, balls of newspaper, sponge balls, disposable cups, paper plates, small boxes, etc. Use any-thing that is safe to handle but you need lots of items. The game can be repeated, passing the items to each other behind their backs or over their heads.

WIND UP 2

Draw the lesson to a conclusion by referring back to the eight special items in the midst of the mass of cereal or paper. Ask the children who were the eight people saved. Noah, his wife, their three sons and their wives. Look at the soggy cereal

(or paper) in the bowl and ask whether they can think who are represented by the 'drowned' cereal. Ask, 'Who saved the eight people and how?' God did by telling Noah to build an ark to escape the flood. The older children could be asked why God saved them. Noah lived in fellowship with God. Explain that, like us feeding animals in the game, Noah and his family would have fed the animals for over a year. Could they play that game for over a year? It is a long time.

GOD CALLS ABRAHAM

Text: Read and study Genesis 11:27 - 12:9

Teaching Point: God chooses people and calls them to follow him.

WARM UP 1

Choose a helper to be the host of the game show, 'Impossible Dreams'. The host may choose to dress up in a glitzy jacket. The object of the game is to select volunteers from the children who would like a dream of theirs to come true. Some dreams may be totally outrageous, some might be very real and heart-rending and some may be profound.

Ask contestant one his or her name, age and the dream that they want to come true. Write the details on a flip-chart. Repeat the process until all the contestants have their dreams recorded. Ask the audience which of these dreams is the most impossible. It may be helpful to prime one of the helpers to become a contestant with a radically impossible dream, e.g. a short person to become the greatest basketball player in the world, a teacher to become an astronaut and discover a new planet, etc. You may not get total agreement as to which one is the most impossible but choose one or more. Can I make the dreams come true? If I promise these contestants that I could give them what they wanted, would they believe me?

Say, 'Today's true story from the Bible is about God making an impossible promise to a man. I want you to find out:

1. Who was the man?
2. What was the promise?
3. Why did it seem impossible?'

(Use the names Abraham and Sarah to avoid any confusion with name changes.)

CONSOLIDATION 1

Tell the children that they are going on a long journey and must carry everything with them. You cannot tell them where they are going to but it is going to be exciting. They have to trust you. Chairs, tables, manageable equipment, boxes, anything safe is suitable. Load up and start purposefully in one direction. Stop after a while and review what Abraham and his family had to do when God told them to leave their home. Journey a little more, then stop and review what promises God made to Abraham. You are now in Haran. Pack up again and move out to another location and make a permanent home with the items you have been carrying. You are now in Canaan. What do you think will happen next? How will Abraham become a great nation? He has no children. It is impossible!

WIND UP 1

Review the answers to the questions from the Warm Up. Remind the children that there are many things that are impossible, but we serve a God who does the impossible everyday. Think about our story and Abraham. God took a 75 year-old man and a 65 year-old woman and told them to travel about 1000 miles, with all their possessions, to a land that God would give them. The land was occupied by another nation, the Canaanites. All of this sounds impossible but it happened. The order was – God commanded, God promised, Abraham obeyed and Abraham was rewarded.

Lesson 4

GOD CALLS ABRAHAM

Text: Read and study Genesis 11:27 - 12:9

Teaching Point: God chooses people and calls them to follow him.

WARM UP 2

God's ways are not man's ways. Place the following instructions in three envelopes, one in each:

1. Sit under a table with your hands on your head and your legs crossed.
2. Lie down motionless on the floor while a leader covers you completely with sheets of newspaper.
3. Tie plastic shopping bags around your feet and keep running on the spot until I tell you to stop.

Choose volunteers from the children and sort them into three groups. Ask each group to choose an envelope and do what the instructions say. The object is to discover if the children will obey the unusual instructions. Some will, some may not. Ask those who refuse why they do not want to follow the command? The children may ask for an explanation as to why they are doing it.

Say that in today's true story from the Bible we will learn about a man, who was called to do something very unusual, just like we asked the volunteers to do today. Will he refuse or will he do what was asked?

CONSOLIDATION 2

The object is to ask the children to perform unusual or pointless tasks that do not appear to make any sense. They may not see them as silly and, even if they do, will probably obey you because you are an authority figure. Abraham was called to do some unusual things that did not make sense, but God said it would be all right in the end. Mark out three or four locations with a bucket at each location. Provide each location with different types of paper, e.g. newspaper, wrapping paper, telephone books, office waste paper, craft paper, old magazines. Send the children to one location and tear the paper there into the smallest pieces possible. Put the pieces into the empty bucket. When all the paper is shredded, direct the children to another location and repeat the process until all the paper is confetti and the buckets are full. Empty the contents of the entire bucket onto a table so the children can see the multitudes of the pieces. Tell the children that the small pieces of paper represent all the descendants Abraham and Sarah were promised by God. There would be so many that they could not be numbered. Abraham and Sarah knew that God's unbelievable promise would come true, because he is the God of the impossible.

WIND UP 2

Remind the children that when God asked Abraham to do something very unusual he did not question, argue, delay or complain. He obeyed God's call and trusted God to do what he promised. If some children refused the Warm Up challenge you could point out how difficult it is to trust people, as some of them have discovered.

LOT'S CHOICE

Text: Read and think about Genesis 13:1-18.

Teaching Point: The importance of making right choices.

WARM UP 1

Place light, bulky items, e.g. cardboard boxes, empty suitcases, large shopping bags filled with paper, in two separate locations. Place a small table in front of the children that will just hold one lot of the bulky items. Instruct the children to collect items from the two separate locations and stack them on the table. No items are to touch the floor. Ensure that it is impossible to put all the items on the table without many of them falling onto the floor. The children may start to argue with each other. Act as peacemaker. Explain that one table is too small and that another table is needed. Arrange for another table to be brought to store the items on. Say, 'In today's true story from the Bible, we will learn how two men sorted out a serious problem. I want you to come back and tell me:

1. The names of the two men.
2. How they sorted out their problem.'

CONSOLIDATION 1

Take three different sheets of coloured card and cut up into rectangles approximately 9 x 5 cm. Issue every child with a piece of coloured card, making sure that there are approximately the same number of each colour. Identify three older children as shepherds and assign each one a colour, telling them how many sheep they have to find. The children are to keep their coloured card hidden from the shepherds. Instruct the children to run around like sheep, feeding, watering and lying down. The three shepherds move amongst the children (sheep), touching them on the head and calling out the shepherd's colour, e.g. red. If the child is carrying a card of that colour, the child follows the shepherd as he goes round looking for the rest of his flock. If the child is not carrying that colour he says, 'Baa' and continues running, grazing, watering, etc. The game continues until the shepherds have collected all their sheep. The first shepherd to finish wins the game. The game can be repeated by changing all the cards, as this will prevent cheating.

WIND UP 1

At the end, review the Warm Up and Consolidation, emphasising that Abraham assessed the problem wisely (overcrowding and not enough food for their livestock), stated the problem clearly, suggested the solution graciously and carried out the solution faithfully. The result was that Abraham was blessed. Lot got the best land but not the best deal (Genesis 13:12-13).

LOT'S CHOICE

Text: Read and think about Genesis 13:1-18.

Teaching Point: The importance of making right choices.

WARM UP 2

The object of the game is to leave the volunteer with the lemon. Provide 12 easy to handle items about the size of a tennis ball or larger and a lemon. Ask for a volunteer from the audience who thinks they make good choices. Place the 13 items on a table in clear view of the audience. Tell the volunteer that the rules are simple. You and the volunteer can choose one, two or three items in turn so that you leave the other person with the lemon at the end. As leader you must always let the volunteer go first. Whatever number they choose, you deduct it from 4 and take that number,

i.e. they choose 1, you choose 3 (= 4)
they choose 2, you choose 2 (= 4)
they choose 3, you choose 1 (= 4).

The volunteer will always be left with the lemon. Repeat as many times as wished, using different volunteers. Even if the game goes wrong and the leader gets left with the lemon, use this to highlight that sometimes we make good decisions and sometimes we make bad ones.

Say, 'Today's true story from the Bible is about a man who had to make a choice.

1. What was his name?
2. What did he choose?
3. Why did he choose it?'

CONSOLIDATION 2

Allocate four locations with a number, letter, colour or compass point. Assemble the children in the centre of these four points and explain to them that when you shout, 'Choose', they are to run to a location and stay there. It can add to the fun if you have a parachute or large sheet of material for them to hide under when they get there. When they are settled at the four locations, declare all the people out at one of the locations. Repeat the process until there is no one left. Restart the game with everyone back in the centre and remind them that they should think carefully about their choices. Sometimes they are good, sometimes they are bad, and sometimes it is just bad luck.

WIND UP 2

Review the questions from the Warm Up. Remind the children that Abraham was thoughtful and gracious in allowing Lot to choose first. It was a good solution to a serious problem. Abraham trusted God to look after his interests and to keep his promise.

GOD KEEPS HIS PROMISE

Text: Read and study Genesis 17:1-8; 18:1-16; 21:1-8

Memory Verse: The Lord is faithful to all his promises. Psalm 145:13

Teaching Point: God keeps his promises and can be trusted.

WARM UP 1

Tell the children, 'If you do (a specified action), I promise to give you a chocolate (or sticker) as a reward'. Younger children can do actions such as jumping 10 times, singing a simple chorus, etc. Each time, keep your promise when the task is completed. Ask the older children to perform more difficult tasks, such as juggling, balancing safe items, press-ups, star jumps, balancing on one leg, imitating famous singers or movie stars, etc. At the completion of each task for the older children, tell them that you have changed your mind, i.e. do not give them anything.

Ask the leaders to do an activity also, such as making a horse (one teacher for front legs and one for back) and carrying a jockey around the room, or hopping the length of the room. On completion say you have changed your mind and will not keep your promise. When you make a second request, prime a teacher to refuse, and when asked why to say, 'Because you cannot be trusted, you do not keep your promise.' Say, 'Today's true story from the Bible is about keeping promises. I want you to come back and tell me:

1. What was the promise?
2. Who made the promise?
3. Why did the man know that the promise would be kept?'

CONSOLIDATION 1

Split the children into equal teams of mixed ages but no more than ten per team. Each team has a list of 10 questions from the Bible passage and the memory verse written out, oone word per sheet of paper, ***'The Lord is faithful to all his promises. Psalm 145:13.'*** Make sure the memory verse sheets are shuffled so they are in the wrong order. If possible, each team's memory verse should be on differently coloured paper. Each team requires a leader to ask the questions. The memory verse sheets are placed in a pile at the far end of the room. The children are asked a question. When the right answer is given, the child runs to the far end, collects one word of the memory verse and returns to base. Only then is the next question asked. Once all ten sheets of paper have been collected, the children put them in the correct order to give the memory verse. The first team to complete the race wins. Questions can be addressed to specific age groups to allow each child in the team to take part.

WIND UP 1

Remind the children how they felt when you did not keep your promise. Tell them that Abraham knew God always keeps his promises. Remind the children that God had previously kept his promise about taking Abraham to a new land. Revise the memory verse.

GOD KEEPS HIS PROMISE

Text: Read and study Genesis 17:1-8; 18:1-16; 21:1-8

Teaching Point: God keeps his promises and can be trusted.

WARM UP 2

Choose three leaders to be examples of trust. Ask the children in the audience to line up behind the leader they trust the most. Ask the children why they chose that one. Listen carefully to their answers. Conduct a test to show that only one of the leaders can be trusted. Provide each of the three leaders with a packet of sweets. In front of the children instruct the leaders to keep the sweets to give to the children after the Bible story. Where should they put them to keep them safe? The trustworthy leader should place the packet in a safe place where the children can see it. The two untrustworthy leaders start to eat their sweets until there are none left. Ask the children if they would like to change their leader for another one. Tell them to do so.

Ask the children why they changed. They started by having faith in their leader, but the leader's actions caused the children to distrust them. Today's true story from the Bible is about God keeping his promise to someone. Send the children off to Bible time with the following questions:

1. Who did God make a promise to?
2. What was the promise?
3. How did the promise come true?

CONSOLIDATION 2

The object of the game is to demonstrate the importance of choosing whom to trust. In the centre of the area place a large collection of safe items, about six per child, e.g. disposable cups, used plastic soft drink containers, plastic jar lids, cardboard boxes or tubs, balls of newspaper, plastic containers, used fruit juice boxes, tennis balls, etc. Appoint three leaders to stand at different points in the room. Prior to the game prime one to be trustworthy and the other two to be unreliable. Instruct the children that on the command, 'Go!' they run to the pile of items, choose one and take it to anyone of the three leaders for safe keeping. They stay with that leader until the next command of 'Go!', when they run and choose another item. When the children go for the next item, the unreliable leaders dispose of the items in their care or throw them back into the centre, so that when the children return there is nothing there. If the children ask where the collected items are, the unreliable leader will say, 'I threw them away'. The children are allowed to change leaders at any stage in the game. See how long it takes for the children to choose another leader who can be trusted.

WIND UP 2

Refer back to the questions from the Warm Up. Remind the children that although some helpers in the Warm Up and Consolidation could not be trusted, one could and that is what the true story from the Bible was about today. God can always be trusted to keep his promises. He will never let us down, and that is what he showed by giving Abraham and Sarah a son, just as he promised.

GOD CARES FOR ISHMAEL

Text: Read and think about Genesis 21:9-21.

Memory verse: The Lord is faithful to all his promises.' Psalm 145 verse 13.

Teaching Point: God cares for his people.

WARM UP 1

You need two telephones and a telephone book, e.g. yellow pages. The leader says, 'I've got a problem. There is a hole in my roof. I need to talk to someone about it.' Find a number in the yellow pages and try talking on the first telephone. There is no answer. Try the other telephone.

There is no answer. Try two other numbers. Still no answer. Say loudly, 'No one heard me! Will no one come to my aid? I am going to drown in oceans of water. I need urgent help now! Please save my goldfish and my old school reports. Is anyone there? Save me from a watery grave, please!'

Say, 'Today's true story from the Bible is about someone who needed help. I want you to come back and tell me:

1. Who needed help?
2. Who helped them?
3. What help was given?'

CONSOLIDATION 1

Divide the children into equal teams. Provide each team with a bucket. At one end of the room make a well from a large cardboard box. Place in the well, at random, a series of approximately nine pictures depicting the Bible story. For older children include one picture that has nothing to do with the story, e.g. an aeroplane, tractor, school bus. The teams start at the end of the room farthest from the well. Direct one child from each team to race to the well with their bucket, pick up a picture and race back to their team. The next child takes the bucket and repeats the action. Continue until all the children have had a turn and collected all the pieces. Instruct the children to put them together chronologically to tell the story.

Required pictures: Ishmael and Isaac, Sarah telling Abraham to send Ishmael away, bag of money (inheritance), Abraham looking sad, skin of water and food, bush, Ishmael crying, an angel and a well. There are many good visual aids books and software packages available to help you produce interesting and quality pictures for games and Warm Ups.

For older children, all the pictures of the story could be placed in one well and the children told that if they collected two pictures of the same, one would have to be returned to the well and exchanged, otherwise they would not be able to collect the set.

WIND UP 1

Review the questions from the Warm Up. Why did God save Ishmael? Because he promised Abraham that he would.

Recite the memory verse.

GOD CARES FOR ISHMAEL

Text: Read and think about Genesis 21:9-21.

Memory verse: The Lord is faithful to all his promises.' Psalm 145 verse 13.

Teaching Point: God cares for his people.

WARM UP 2

The object of the presentation is to show conspicuous care for one person while ignoring the other one. Invite two male volunteers from the audience to pretend to be brothers. One should be a child and one a leader, recognising that Ishmael was about 14 years older than Isaac (Genesis 16:15-16; 21:5). The contrast is more important than the numeric difference. Inform the audience that the boys are brothers. Provide the younger child with lots of attractively wrapped pretend presents. Produce them one or two at a time and build up a big pile. All the presents could be produced out of a sack or box and be labelled, 'For the younger brother', or similar. As the presents are handed out console the older brother with the words, 'I am sure there will be something for you'. When all the presents are distributed and the older brother has none, offer him some bread and a glass of water. 'This is all I have for you.'

In today's true story from the Bible, we'll learn about two brothers who had to be separated. Listen very carefully and come back later and tell me:

1. Who were the brothers?
2. Who were their mothers?
3. How did God care for the older one?

CONSOLIDATION 2

The object of this game is to allow the children to demonstrate that they care for someone by helping them out. Create a huge mess in one part of the meeting area. Old clean clothes, shirts, socks, trousers etc. can be placed in a pile and covered with newspaper to hide them. Place random chairs, furniture, etc. on and around the pile of clothes and newspapers. Empty cardboard boxes & plastic drink bottles can be added to the pile also. Point out to the children that this mess has to be cleared up, otherwise you will have to stay on for a long time and you are very tired. Will they help you? Make a challenge out of this mundane task.

Assign one group of the children to fold the clothing. Another group to collect the newspapers and put them back in page order. Another group could sort out the furniture, boxes etc. The task requires speed and neatness. Allocate separate areas for the children to sort, fold and stack so they do not get in each other's way. Judge each area and assign marks out of ten. Find something praiseworthy about each group.

WIND UP 2

Thank the children for caring enough to help you sort out the mess. Review the questions from the Warm Up. Ask who was in trouble in today's true story from the Bible. Who cared for them? How did God care for them? Remind the children that God cares for all his people and we can always depend on him to know everything that is happening to us and to do what is right.

GOD PROVIDES

Text: Genesis 22:1-19

Teaching Point: God should be put first and obeyed even when it is hard to do so.

WARM UP 1

Invite a friend to show you a valuable possession of theirs. Make sure that it is an item that appears to be valuable to the children also, e.g. money box, jewellery, camera, hobby item, roller skates, a popular storybook, a toy, football kit, favourite clothing, etc. Have the friend go on for a few minutes about how good the item is, while you become enamoured of the item. The children should understand that this is one of the most important things in this person's life. Touch the item, admire it, hold it up against you if it is clothing or something to wear. Show clearly that it is something that you would want for yourself.

Ask the friend, 'How long have we been friends? How much do you like me?' Build it up so that it is clear you are the very best friend there is. Now ask your friend, 'Would you show how much you love me by giving me your most valuable possession?' Your friend thinks long and hard, then says that, while they like you a lot, what you are asking is very hard. The friend hesitates, then offers something else instead of the item you want. No, it has to be that treasure (point to it). Your friend says, 'May I think about it?'

Say, 'Today's true story from the Bible is about someone who was asked to do something very hard. Come back after the story and tell me:

1. Who was the man?
2. Who asked the man to do the hard thing?
3. What did the man have to do?
4. How did it turn out?'

CONSOLIDATION 1

Liberally scatter obstacles around so that there is no easy path from one place to another. Divide the children into teams, each with a leader. Ask for volunteers to be blindfolded. Blindfold the children and hand in hand the leader guides them through the minefield, talking to them and avoiding the obstacles. Do not force children to put on a blindfold. After each child has had a turn, reverse the process so that they guide the leader.

WIND UP 1

For those children who took part in crossing the minefield blindfolded, ask them why they agreed to be led across. Their answer will probably be because they trusted their leader. For those who did not take part it will be because they were afraid or did not trust their leader. Review the questions from the Warm Up. We can trust God to look after us in all things, just as he did in the story of Abraham and Isaac.

GOD PROVIDES

Text: Genesis 22:1-19

Teaching Point: God should be put first and obeyed even when it is hard to do so.

WARM UP 2

The following Warm Up should be done as a skit or using puppets. (see page 86)

The leader is standing by the table when a friend arrives. The friend asks if the special item has arrived. He has been waiting a whole year for it. He asks if it is the colour he wanted, if it is the most up-to-date model, etc. The leader answers each query in the affirmative. The leader eventually produces the item and places it on the table. The friend is delighted with the item and wants it straight away. The leader says that, unfortunately, there is a problem. The leader needs to take the item back at the end of the session - for ever. The friend is horrified and protests volubly.

Leader: 'If you love me, you will trust me and do as I ask. In today's true story from the Bible we will learn about someone who was asked to give up his most precious thing.

1. Who had to give up something precious?
2. What did the person have to give up?
3. What happened?'

CONSOLIDATION 2

Place all the children in a large circle, or if space is limited, an inner and an outer circle. The children can sit or stand. If using two circles, the inner circle could stand while the outer circle sits. Rotate after the game ends.

Give six children at random a small soft ball or sponge block. On the command, 'Go!', the children hand the ball to the person on their left (clockwise) and the process is repeated until the leader says, 'Stop!' Whoever is caught with the ball is out and must take their ball into the centre of the circle. Ask the children in the circle who are not out, 'Who will agree to take any of these persons' places?' If you have any volunteers, substitute them for the person(s) in the centre. Any child returning to circle takes their ball with them. Provide another six soft items at random to children in the circle and repeat the process. If you have a small number of children only use one, two or three items each time. Repeat until there are no children left.

Note the key to the game. All the children who were out should have a ball and those who agreed to substitute for a child will not have a ball. These are the real winners, so give them a real reward for taking the place of another. Obviously, once you have done this once, the older children will fathom that they can win (get a reward) by substituting themselves for someone who is out. Repeat the game from the beginning, reversing the direction and this time providing bigger items but still soft, e.g. soft cushions, bin liners with paper in them, bean bags, shopping bags with rolled up newspaper, sponge rubber footballs, balloons if appropriate.

WIND UP 2

Review the questions from the Warm Up. Remind the children that, because Abraham trusted God, even with the life of his son, God provided a substitute, and his son Isaac was saved.

GOD GUIDES

Text: Read and study Genesis 24:1-67.

Teaching Point: God guides those who obey him.

Lesson 9

WARM UP 1

The object is to devise a test to select one child from a larger group. Provide seven different items (e.g. toys, shoes, cereal boxes, hats, sports equipment, etc.) and display them on a table up front. Choose seven volunteers to come forward and choose one item each. When they have chosen the item, reveal the winning item by showing a card or sheet of paper with the appropriate shape on it e.g. toy car. The person who chose the toy car stays out in front, the other volunteers return to the group and you ask for another seven volunteers. Choose a different item, e.g. a doll. Repeat the process three or four times, leaving the winners at the front each time. Now take the winners and have a final test to see who chooses the item displayed. This person is the grand winner. After the children return to the group, the leader says, 'In today's true story from the Bible, someone used a test to decide an important question. I want you to tell me:

1. What test was used?
2. The special thing that this test was used to find.'

CONSOLIDATION 1

Water the Camels. The object of the game is for the children to take 'water' from a well and fill up a trough for the camels to drink. Use polystyrene packing shapes used to protect goods packed in cardboard boxes, or small balls of newspaper for water. Divide the group into teams of equal numbers and provide each team with a plastic bucket full of 'water'. Also provide each team with a small cup to carry the 'water' from the well to the trough. The trough can be a cardboard box large enough to take the contents of all the plastic buckets. Place the cardboard box equidistant from the teams. On the command, 'Go!' the first person in each team dips the cup into the plastic bucket of 'water', fills it up with one hand only and carries the contents to the cardboard box where they tip it out. Do not allow the children to place the free hand over the top of the cup. The person returns to the team, hands the cup to the next child who fills and empties it. Repeat the process until the plastic bucket is completely empty. The team to empty its plastic bucket first, wins. Say, 'Boy, those camels sure hold a lot of water!'

WIND UP 1

Review the questions from the Warm Up. Remind the children of how Rebekah watered the camels, just as they did in the game. Today we learnt how God guides his people, sometimes in very strange ways. We can always trust God to guide us in ways that are right, even if they are sometimes unusual. That doesn't mean we should put God to silly tests to prove he guides us. Testing is God's job, not ours.

GOD GUIDES

Text: Read and study Genesis 24:1-67.

Teaching Point: God guides those who obey him.

WARM UP 2

The object is to introduce 13 words, four of which will feature in the Bible lesson that follows. Prepare a set of 12 question cards plus a set of 13 answer cards. Pin the answer cards onto a board. Ask for six volunteers and ask them one at a time, the following questions in any order you like, pinning up the question on the board. The volunteer chooses an answer from the answer cards on the pin board. If a humorous answer is suggested, play along and pin the answer against the question.

1. What do you eat for breakfast?
2. Which animal can go for a long time without water?
3. What do you wear on your feet?
4. What flies in the sky?
5. What do you eat with tea or coffee?
6. What lives in your garden?
7. What do you bathe in?
8. What do you put on your cornflakes?
9. Where do you draw water from?
10. Where do you put earthworms for safekeeping?
11. Where do you put schoolbooks?
12. What is a popular English summer game?

Answer cards: aeroplane, camels, cornflakes, cricket, doughnuts, earthworms, jar, milk, orange juice, schoolbag, trainers, water, well.

Leader: 'In today's true story from the Bible, only four of these words will be mentioned. Listen carefully to this exciting story and come back and tell me which are the correct words.'

CONSOLIDATION 2

Divide the group into equal teams of mixed ability. Place the answer cards from the Warm Up in the centre of the teams. The object of the game is to send one person at a time to pick up one card and return home, before the next person goes and collects another card. Repeat until there are no cards left. When everyone is seated, declare the winners to be the team with the 'jar' card. Remove this card from the game and place it on a pin board in full sight of the group. Repeat the procedure removing the well, water and camels cards at the end of each round. These cards comprise the answers to the questions from the Warm Up and should be used to wind up the day's teachings (see below). The children may have already worked out the object of the game and deliberately go looking for the right card. If this is so, throw in a dummy winner, like earthworms, and remove it at the Wind Up stage.

WIND UP 2

Review the questions and answers from the Warm Up. Remind the children that the test set by Abraham's servant was a very unusual (strange) test, but God listened to him and made it come true. God does sometimes work in unusual ways. He also works in ordinary ways and we should acknowledge these as well. The choosing of Isaac's wife, Rebekah, was truly remarkable and amazing.

JACOB DECEIVING

Text: Read and study Genesis 25:19-34; 26:34 - 27:41.

Teaching Point: Deceit and selfishness always lead to unhappiness and displease God.

WARM UP 1

Collect four empty chocolates or sweets boxes. Fill the boxes with items that sound like chocolates in a box and weigh about the same. The boxes should appear as new and unopened as possible. These boxes will be the prizes for the quiz. Two object lessons will be taught. The first is deceiving, because the children will think that the boxes contain chocolates and not stones or other rubbish. The second is that you will choose the same person each time to answer the questions and thereby demonstrate favouritism. Ask the children four questions from last week's story or a recent series you have been teaching. Choose someone who will know the answers or who has been given the answers before the session. Let them choose a box of chocolates after each question is answered correctly. The children will start to get annoyed after the second prize goes to the same person. Ask them why they are so angry. They will say that it is not fair. When all four boxes are handed over ask the winner to open them and share the contents. They will be further disappointed that they have been deceived. First favouritism, followed by deceit. Leader: 'Come back after your story and tell me what happened in today's true story from the Bible that also happened in the Warm Up.'

CONSOLIDATION 1

Place four leaders at four points in the room. The children sit in a circle in the centre. The leaders have to convince the children to join them. At each turn only one leader is genuine, the other three are imposters. On the command 'Go!' all the leaders invite the children to join their group. The children have 30 seconds to decide which leader to join. When all the children are in groups nominate the legitimate leader. All children in that group stay in the game but those in the other three groups were deceived and are out. The winners return to the centre and the process is repeated. This time choose another leader to be the non-deceiver. Do this at random or logically (clockwise/anticlockwise). Repeat until only one child is left. Restart the process if time allows.

WIND UP 1

Ask these questions and draw out the answers given.

1. What happened in the Warm Up that also happened in the story today? *We were deceived by you, and Isaac was deceived by Jacob and Rebekah.*
2. Did you like me when I deceived you? *No, it was a very unkind thing to do.*
3. When the leaders tricked you into joining them in the game, was that fair? *No. Reinforce the truth that we must never deceive people because it only causes hurt in the end.*
4. What else happened in the story that we saw in the Warm Up? *Favouritism. Isaac preferred Esau and Rebekah preferred Jacob.* Reinforce the truth that we must treat everyone the same, because that is how God treats us. Isaac and Rebekah were wrong.

JACOB DECEIVING

Text: Read and study Genesis 25:19-34; 26:34 - 27:41.

Teaching Point: Deceit and selfishness always lead to unhappiness and displease God.

WARM UP 2

The leader enters and explains to everyone that he has a special present for a very special friend. He displays the gift, a large beautifully wrapped box. Another person, who has been primed beforehand, enters and is warmly greeted by the leader, who explains that this is a very, very special friend. The friend sees the gift and walks around it admiringly. He says that since it is so attractive, it must be for a very special person. The leader tells him that it is and that it is for him. The friend is overjoyed and thanks the leader profusely. They may even exchange hugs if appropriate. The leader gives the gift to the friend who proceeds to open it. As he takes off the box, he looks at the audience with deep disappointment written on his face. 'Oh! It's empty!' he cries. The leader bursts out laughing and turns to the children, saying, 'Wasn't that some trick I played on him?'

Say, 'In today's true story from the Bible we will find out what happened when some people cheated someone. I want you to find out the answers to the following questions:

1. Who was cheated?
2. Who did the cheating?
3. How was the person cheated?
4. How did the people feel about being cheated?'

CONSOLIDATION 2

Divide the children into four equal teams and place them at the four points around the edge of the room. Allocate a colour to each team and provide each team with at least eight items of their colour. At the centre of the room place a sheet or parachute. The object of the game is to get rid of all your coloured items and to collect all the items of a different colour. (This will require cunning, deceit and perhaps some cheating.) Tell the children that there will be a big prize for the winners. On the command, 'Lose', the team members run into the centre, deposit their coloured items onto the sheet and return to their place. Remember, a team cannot win if it keeps one or more items of its original colour, so they will probably unload the lot at the first opportunity. Teams can now work out what colour they should collect. On the command 'Collect', everyone races into the centre to collect as many of one colour as possible, but not their own. Good strategy will make the game interesting, but children will generally just opt for one colour to win quickly. Repeat the process 'lose' and 'collect' until one team has changed its original colour for another. If the children cheat or deceive one another, remind them about the true story from the Bible and how tricking or cheating made people very unhappy, even angry, with one another. Repeat the game as long as time and interest allow. Remind the children that there is a big prize for the winners at the end, but not now. The children should start to smell a rat from the way the leader deceived them in the Warm Up.

WIND UP 2

Remind the children of what happened in the Warm Up. Do they think that the winning team in the game will get the offered prize? Review the answers to the questions from the Warm Up. Point out that deceit causes great unhappiness and remind them of their disappointment at not receiving what was offered. God is not pleased when we deceive other people.

JACOB DREAMING

Text: Read and study Genesis 27:42 - 28:22.

Teaching Point: God always keeps his promises.

WARM UP 1

Advise the group that you have promised to keep the room clean. Provide the children with brush, brooms and dustpans. Ask them to see if you have kept your promise. Ask them to collect as much dust as they can find in a few minutes. All rooms have dust somewhere, but you may choose to empty a vacuum cleaner bag into a newspaper to show how fine dust can be. Some skirting boards collect dust so you could run your finger along one to collect some. Place the dust particles on an OHP so that everyone can see them. Provide some sand or sugar samples for the children to find.

Say, 'Today's true story from the Bible is about a promise and some dust. Come back after the Bible story and tell me what they had to do with each other (Genesis 28:14).'

CONSOLIDATION 1

Divide the group into teams and issue them with two or three newspapers. Ask them to tear the newspapers into the smallest pieces possible and place the confetti edge to edge in a straight line. The team with the longest line wins. A time limit on this exercise is recommended so that the children have time to count the pieces. Once all the pieces are counted, combine all the team pieces into one big pile.

WIND UP 1

Remind the group about the dust they collected in the Warm Up. What did this have to do with the true story from the Bible today? The descendants of Jacob would be as numerous as the specks of dust on the earth (Genesis 28:14). Link in to the multitude of scraps of paper from the game. God promised that Jacob's descendents would be many, many more than that. Point out that you could not keep your promise to keep the room clean, because the dust is so small and there is so much of it. But God always keeps his promises and, over the next few weeks they will see just how God began to keep his promise to Jacob.

JACOB DREAMING

Text: Read and study Genesis 27:42 - 28:22.

Teaching Point: God's purposes cannot be thwarted.

WARM UP 2

The object is to find out how many ways the children know of getting a message from one person to another. The following is a checklist:

Letter, e-mail, telephone, carrier pigeon, telegram, Morse code, radio broadcast, fax, semaphore, smoke signals, jungle drums, an ad in a newspaper, message on Teletext or TV programmes, notice-board, word of mouth.

Record the suggestions on a flip-chart or white board, or display pictures of the different ways for the children to find and pin up on a board. When the list is comprehensive, say to the children, 'There is still one missing.' Leaders may make some suggestions. Say, 'There is still one missing. In today's true story from the Bible we will learn how God had a special way of communicating with (getting a message to) people. Please listen carefully to the Bible lesson and come back and tell me the special way God used.'

CONSOLIDATION 2

The object of the game is for the children to try to frustrate your plans. You will make a series of messes, which they will clear up as quickly as possible, collecting as many items as possible in teams of four or five children. Each team is awarded a point for each item collected. For example, spread 30 plastic bottle tops on the floor. One person from each team rushes out, collects one item and returns to the team before the next person goes. Repeat until all items are collected. If the children are all the same age or size or skill levels, you can let them all go at the same time, but emphasise that there is to be no rough play. Count up the items, award points and place the collected items into a box or bucket near to you. Spread 50 building blocks on the floor and repeat the process. Spread 20 sponges or kitchen towel cardboard cylinders.

Recycle the plastic bottle tops and the building blocks on the floor and repeat the process. Put all the items on the floor and repeat the process. You made a mess (plan) and the children cleaned it up. Who was going to win? The person who made the mess or the people who cleaned up? By recycling the items you will always win because after the items are counted for each round, a new mess is made and it goes on until you call a stop, preferably with uncollected items still on the floor, showing that they have been unable to thwart your plan. Leaders can help clear up the mess, but do not let the children make the mess for you or your leaders to clear up.

WIND UP 2

Review the question from the Warm Up. How did God get his message to Jacob? In a dream. Remind them that they were unable to win the game. When you said, 'Stop!' there were still items uncollected on the floor. We can never overturn or change God's plans; they always come true. God always keeps his plans and promises. God reminded Jacob of that in today's true story from the Bible. He said that he would keep his promise to Abraham about his descendants being as numerous as the dust on the earth. This is how it is going to be and that is exactly what happened. Jacob set God a test. Would that stop God's plan for him? No! God's plans cannot be thwarted.

JACOB DECEIVED

Text: Read and study Genesis 29:1 - 30:43.

Teaching Point: God starts to fulfil his promises to Jacob.

WARM UP 1

The object is to start a picture, but leave it incomplete so that it looks incomprehensible. Being drawn upside down will further complicate it. Prior to the meeting very lightly draw in pencil an enlarged shape or picture onto a flip-chart or large sheet of paper. Do this by photocopying an image onto an acetate sheet of film and then projecting the image onto the flip-chart using the overhead projector. Pictures can include that of animals, boys or girls playing a game, landscape, a farmyard or a suitable cartoon character. Using giant marker pens, start to fill in some of the lines and shapes on the picture. The children can volunteer which colours to use. At a suitable point ask the children to guess what the picture is.

Say, 'I've started to draw this picture and it's a bit difficult to see what it is about because it is not finished. In today's true story from the Bible we will discover how God started to fulfil some of his promises to Jacob, even though Jacob couldn't see the whole picture of what God was doing. Please come back and tell me how God started to fulfil some of his promises to Jacob.'

If you are not artistic, a large jigsaw can be used instead. For older children you could take the poster of a popular figure the children will know and cut it into puzzle pieces. Display the less obvious pieces but only reveal half of the image. Ask the children to guess what it might be.

CONSOLIDATION 1

God started to fulfil his promises to Jacob by giving him 11 sons and one daughter (Benjamin was not yet born). Jacob also acquired herds and wealth to sustain his large family. The object of the Consolidation is to find 11 items of the same description while you produce one of another description. The children can also be asked to do 11 exercises (aerobics) while you do one. Items to find can include the following:

- 11 newspapers, magazines or books,
- 11 disposable cups
- 11 boxes
- 11 toys
- 11 chairs
- 11 felt tipped pens or colouring pencils
- 11 shoes
- 11 bottle caps
- 11 drinking straws.

Suggestions for exercises:

- 11 hops
- 11 skips
- 11 frog jumps
- 11 star jumps
- 11 press-ups
- 11 sit-ups
- 11 touch your toes standing
- 11 touch your toes sitting
- 11 squats.

WIND UP 1

Return to the picture you started at the beginning. Let's go back to it and see if we can make sense of it. Add a piece at a time and ask the children what it is. Refer back to the story of Jacob and how God started to fulfil his promises to him. How did he do that? By giving him 11 sons (Benjamin had not yet been born) and one daughter. Can you remember the games we played? They were all about 11 and one. After the children what came next? The flocks, slaves, camels and donkeys. This was just the start of how God would keep his promises to Jacob. God makes many promises to his people; some of those promises are completed but others are still to be fulfilled. God always keeps his promises.

JACOB DECEIVED

Text: Read and study Genesis 29:1 - 30:43.

Teaching Point: God starts to fulfil his promises to Jacob.

WARM UP 2

Ask a volunteer to come to the front of the class and tell him that you will give him 10,000 of any item you can easily obtain. (You will not have to actually find 10,000 of any item, so don't worry!) Items can include sweets, bottle caps, pictures, etc. Give him 11 of the promised item. Ask the rest of the class, 'Do you think that I will give him the rest of the 10,000?' Repeat the process with one or two more children as time permits, varying the number promised but always giving the volunteer 11 of what was promised and asking the same question at the end.

Say, 'In today's true story from the Bible, someone who was promised a lot of something was given a part of the promise. When you come back I want you to tell me:

1. Who the person was.
2. What he was promised.
3. What part of the promise was fulfilled in today's story.'

CONSOLIDATION 2

The object of the game is to collect 11 items from a central location before the other teams do. Divide the children into four equal teams and place them at four corners of the room. In the centre place a number of items in groups of 11, e.g. 11 disposable cups, 11 bottle caps, 11 plastic straws, etc. A member of each team runs to the centre, chooses an object, returns to the team, places the object in full view of everyone and tags the next person to repeat the exercise.

Teams will probably choose the same items and therefore will not be able to complete their 11 objects unless they change objects or take objects from the other teams, which they are allowed to do. Teams are not allowed to stop other teams from taking one of the objects they have collected. The strategy is to get one of each object to start with so the other teams cannot win then to start collecting the objects the team thinks it can win with. This game can go on forever; it will start but not end. To speed the game up or bring it to a conclusion, instruct the teams to collect two, three, four or five objects at a time, which will cause chaos. Remind the children at the end that the story about Jacob was about the start of a promise coming true. That promise is still happening today. Jacob's descendants are like the dust on the earth. We will learn later of other parts of the promise God made to Jacob.

WIND UP 2

Ask the children whether they remembered the name of the man that God had made a promise to. [*Jacob.*] Ask whether they remembered what the promise was. [*I will give to you and your descendants this land on which you are lying. They will be as numerous as the specks of dust on the earth. Through you and your descendants I will bless all the nations.*] You do not have to get each bit of the promise, but stay with them until they get to the bit about many descendants. Stick pictures onto a board to represent each part of the promise that they remember. Ask which part of the promise was fulfilled in today's lesson. Tell the children that this was another example of God keeping his promises.

JACOB TRUSTING GOD

Text: Genesis 31:1-3; 32:1 - 33:20

Teaching Point: There is no need to be afraid if God is with you.

WARM UP 1

Either a skit or puppets (see puppet script on page 87). Toby appears with a dismembered soft toy in his hand. He looks furtively left, right, up and down. Guilt is evident. He asks the audience if they have seen Trudy and explains that he borrowed her favourite toy while she was out. While he was playing with it, this is what happened (shows toy to audience). Trudy arrives and realises something is wrong. Toby tries to placate her, but she is suspicious and says she will talk it over with her favourite toy. She asks Toby if he has seen it. Toby replies, 'No', and tries to distract her with gifts. Trudy notices the toy dangling from Toby's hand and that it has the same colours as her missing toy, but does not immediately make the connection. Eventually Trudy realises it is her toy and threatens Toby. The leader intervenes and draws the skit to a close.

Leader says, 'In today's true story from the Bible we will find out what happened when someone tried to use gifts to gain acceptance. I want you to tell me afterwards:

1. Who offered a huge gift to get acceptance?
2. Who was the gift offered to?
3. Why did he offer the gift?'

CONSOLIDATION 1

The object of this game is to collect items that represent the gift Jacob gave to Esau. Each team requires five herds, consisting of coloured silhouettes, with a different colour for each herd (see diagrams on page 32).

Herd 1: 200 female goats and 20 male ones, two goat silhouettes with '100' written on each and two with '10' written on each.

Herd 2: 200 female sheep and 20 male sheep, two sheep silhouettes with '100' written on each and two with '10' written on each.

Herd 3: 30 female camels with calves, 2 camel silhouettes with '15' written on each.

Herd 4: 40 cows and 10 bulls, two cow silhouettes with '20' written on each and two bull silhouettes with '5' written on each.

Herd 5: 20 female donkeys and 10 male donkeys, two donkey silhouettes with '10' written on each and two with '5' written on each.

Place the five groups of cards in separate locations. Give each team a colour to collect. One person from each team runs out, collects an animal shape and returns to the start before the next person goes. Repeat until all shapes are collected. The first team with a full set wins. If time and enthusiasm allow, repeat by changing the team colours.

WIND UP 1

Review the questions from the Warm Up and remind the children that God was always in control, even though Jacob was afraid and distressed. Remind the children of the game. How many of each animal did Jacob give to Esau? Jacob's trust in God was not absolute in spite of the signs God had given him. Everything turned out well, even though Jacob didn't display unqualified trust, because God was with him.

JACOB TRUSTING GOD

Text: Genesis 31:1-3; 32:1 - 33:20

Teaching Point: There is no need to be afraid if God is with you.

WARM UP 2

Prepare a collection of greeting cards or gift wrapping paper that shows a variety of celebrations. Also have a collection of gift-wrapped boxes of varying sizes. Ask the children to name some occasions when we give or receive presents. Display the card, wrapping paper or gift that corresponds to their response. The suggestions may include such celebrations as Easter (show Easter egg), birthday (show gift), wedding (show toaster), Christmas (show box wrapped in Christmas wrapping), etc. At the end put the gifts in order of size, going from small to large. Say, 'In today's true story from the Bible we will learn about a gift that was so big it wouldn't fit into this room. Please come back and tell me:

1. What the gift was.
2. Who gave it.
3. Who it was given to and why.'

CONSOLIDATION 2

Prepare a set of celebration cards, wrapping paper and gifts for each team. The cards, gifts and wrapping paper need not be new. You will also need tape, ribbons and/or paste or glue.

The object of the game is for the children to collect a card, wrapping paper and gift that comprise a set. Once they have the three items they wrap the gift up, address the card to Esau and sign it as from Jacob. Younger children will need help from a leader or older child. For difficult to wrap items, e.g. soft toy, a plastic shopping bag or box could be used with paper wrapped round the outside.

Distribute the cards, wrapping paper and gifts over as large an area as possible. Divide the children into teams of three. On the command, 'Go!' one person from each team goes to the items and chooses one, e.g. a birthday card. When they return to the team, the next person collects the wrapping paper and the third the gift that goes with the card and paper. If the wrong gift is chosen, the leader must direct the child to return it to the collection area and choose the right one. This also applies to the card and paper if the gift is chosen first. The first team to wrap the gift and address the card wins a point. Repeat until all the items are used.

WIND UP 2

Talk about the importance of getting the gift right. Review the questions from the Warm Up. Did Jacob get the gift right? Remind the children that God was always in control, even though Jacob was afraid and distressed. His trust of God was not absolute in spite of the signs God had given him. Everything turned out well, even though Jacob didn't display unqualified trust.

JOSEPH HATED BY HIS BROTHERS

Text: Read and study Genesis 37:1-36.

Teaching Point: To discover what happens when family relationships go wrong.

WARM UP 1

Prior to the Warm Ip, prime a leader to do anything they wish while the obedience game is being played. Under no circumstances will they be out; you will show them unlimited favouritism. The object of the Warm Up is to see how the children react to blatant favouritism. Will they be like Joseph's brothers and hate him more and more, or will they be tolerant and forgiving? Either reaction will be an effective way into the Bible story.

Tell the children that you are going to play an obedience game called, 'Sit, Stand or Statues'. The rules are simple. When you say, 'Stand', everyone stands up. The last person to stand up, or anyone who does not stand up, is out of the game. When you say, 'Sit', everyone sits. The last person to sit, or to stay standing up, is out. When you say, 'Statues', everyone remains motionless until the next command is shouted out. While this is going on your favourite will do anything he wishes and not be counted out. If the children complain, explain that this person is your very best friend and will never get out. Declare your friend the winner. Ask the children how they feel when someone is being favoured. How do they feel about the person showing the favouritism, about the person being favoured, and about each other? Say, 'In today's true story from the Bible you will discover how a family was affected by favouritism. I want you to come back and tell me:

1. Who showed favouritism?
2. Who was favoured?
3. How did the brothers react?'

CONSOLIDATION 1

The object of the game is to favour one team over the others. The game is called 'House on Fire'. Divide the group into teams of about 10-12 children, ensuring that the younger children are in a separate team from the older ones. Each team needs a collection of items that can be moved safely from one place to another by being passed from child to child in a line. Provide larger items for the bigger children and light items for the younger ones. Tell the children that their house is on fire and each team must move their items from the house to safety. Ensure that the youngest team wins by favouring them. They should have fewer items and smaller ones than everyone else, and they can run or carry their items whereas everyone else must hand the item to the next person without moving their feet.

A prize (preferably edible) could be offered to wind up the emotional stakes and reinforce the consequences of favouritism. At the end of the game, if time permits, you can ask the children to return the items from the safe zone back into their house. Once again the chosen favourite will win, irrespective of how fast they are.

WIND UP 1

Review the questions from the Warm Up. Emphasise that Jacob was wrong to favour Joseph over his other children, because it caused bad feelings, which led to hatred of Joseph. Remind the children of their feelings in the game when the youngest group was favoured. Joseph was also foolish in the way that he behaved towards his brothers and parents. It was not a very happy family, but God was still in control, working out his perfect plans through very imperfect people and situations. If a prize was given in the game, distribute something to the rest of the group.

Chocolate

JOSEPH HATED BY HIS BROTHERS

Text: Read and study Genesis 37:1-36.

Teaching Point: To discover what happens when family relationships go wrong.

WARM UP 2

The object of the Warm Up is for six volunteers to try and get rid of three large objects without leaving a small defined area. Mark out three squares large enough to hold two volunteers and a large cardboard box. Ask for six volunteers and place two in each square with the largest lightweight cardboard box you can find (or similar). The volunteers have to get rid of the box completely, without leaving the small square. They are not allowed to throw any of the box away. They may try to squash, compress, tear or destroy the box and hide the pieces on their person. The right response is to give the box to someone in the audience and ask them to take it away and hide it. Do not help them in any way, but remind them of the rules. The box has to disappear but the volunteers are not to leave the square or throw the box.

Say, 'In today's true story from the Bible some people wanted to get rid of something they hated. Come back and tell me:

1. Who they were.
2. What did they want to get rid of?
3. How did they do it?'

CONSOLIDATION 2

The object of the game is to collect cut-out shapes of details from the story and paste them into a collage. You will need the following shapes: two Josephs, Jacob, 11 brothers, camels, sun, moon, 11 stars, 11 small sheaves, one big sheaf, one dry well, 20 pieces of silver (foil covered circles), one brightly coloured robe with long sleeves, sheep. You should have about 70 items. See page 33

Hide the shapes in reasonably easy to find locations. Instruct the children to find all the shapes and paste them onto a large piece of card or paper, such as a length of wallpaper. Prepare this beforehand by tracing around the shapes in pencil, so the children will know where to glue the pieces they find. The end result should be a repeat of the Bible story.

WIND UP 2

Review the questions from the Warm Up with the children, referring back to the right way to get rid of the box. Use the collage to review the details of the Bible story. Do they really think God was in control when Joseph's brothers sold him to the Ishmaelite traders who took him to Egypt? Next time we will find out some more strange things that happened to Joseph and whether God was still in control.

JOSEPH IMPRISONED IN EGYPT

Text: Read and study Genesis 39:1 – 40: 23

Teaching Point: God was with Joseph in every situation.

WARM UP 1

Prior to the Warm Up, prime a leader to falsely accuse you of stealing their expensive watch. You could be dressed to look like a successful person. Prepare an area to look like a prison, such as a cardboard box with bars cut out that can be placed over the head or a curtain or sheet with a square section cut out, or have play handcuffs ready to be used.

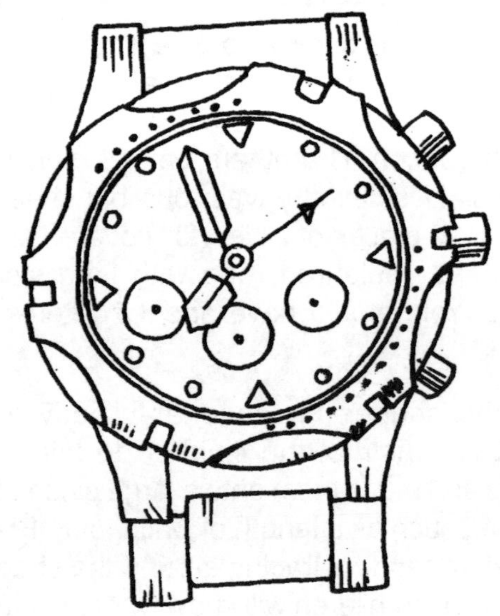

Start by saying, 'I have a very important job and I am very good at it. I work for an important man, who trusts me with everything he owns. I do everything he asks. I am going to hire three people to help me with my job. Who would like to work for me? You must be honest and ready to work hard. Now, volunteers stand up!'

Before the choosing takes place, the accuser comes in and says that his expensive watch has been stolen. Nobody must leave the room while he makes a search. Instruct the children to look around and see if they can find the missing watch. Allow a minute or so for the search. Tell the accuser that you can't find it. The accuser then remembers that the leader was in his house earlier and was left alone in the same room as the watch. The leader agrees that this was the case. The accuser says, 'Means, opportunity, motive. Arrest that person and throw him into prison.' Leader (from the prison), 'Today's true story from the Bible is about a man who was accused of doing something and thrown into prison. I want you to come back and tell me:

1. Who was he?
2. Who accused him?
3. Who put him into prison?
4. Did he do what he was accused of?'

CONSOLIDATION 1

The children are put into 'prison', where they have to sort out the Bible verse, 'the Lord was with Joseph and made him succeed in everything that he did (Genesis 39:23 GNB).' When the older children have put the verse into the correct order everyone gets out of prison. The younger children, who cannot read, must trust and wait for the older ones to get it right, just as Joseph had to wait patiently for God to arrange things to get him out of prison. Divide the children into multi-age teams and arrange one prison area for each team. Place a set of cards containing the Bible verse, one word to each card, in jumbled order in each prison. On the command, 'Go to Prison!' the teams rush to their defined area and sort the 14 pieces of card into verse order. Once this has been accomplished the team are allowed out of prison. The first team to get free wins.

WIND UP 1

Review the questions from the Warm Up. Remind the children that bad things happened to Joseph last week, asking them what these were, and things do not seem to be getting any better this week. Joseph is in prison and has been forgotten. Ask the children to repeat the Bible verse that got them out of prison. God was always with Joseph, at Dothan, in the well, on the way to Egypt, in Potiphar's house and in prison, protecting him and working his purposes out.

JOSEPH IMPRISONED IN EGYPT

Text: Read and study Genesis 39:1 – 40: 23

Teaching Point: God was with Joseph in every situation.

WARM UP 2

The object of the Warm Up is for the children to identify the jobs associated with clothing, tools and equipment and to remember which ones were mentioned in the story. Display a selection of items such as a builder's hard hat and shovel / hammer / saw, a policeman's hat and truncheon, a cowboy hat and rope, a butcher's white hat, striped apron and meat items, a baker's hat and bread, a wine steward's jacket and tray with bottle and glasses, a boilersuit or overalls and spanners, a cleaner's apron, mop and bucket, a pair of jeans and checked shirt for a farmer with a bag of seed or bucket for chicken feed.

Place the clothes on one side and the equipment on the other. Ask the children to choose an item of clothing and the equipment that goes with it. When they get it right ask them to come out to the front and put them on. If they are shy they can nominate a leader to put on those items. Make sure the baker and wine steward are chosen and displayed up front. Say, 'In today's true story from the Bible only two of these jobs are mentioned. Come back and tell me which they were.'

CONSOLIDATION 2

The object of the game is to see which group of children makes the best wine stewards and bakers, by carrying unstable items. Divide the group into three or four teams. Provide each team with two trays or sheets of cardboard. On one tray place empty plastic soft drink bottles and three disposable cups. On the second tray place six tennis balls, table tennis balls or other round items to represent bread baked by the baker. The stewards and bakers have to walk to a set point and return, without spilling the contents of their trays. Two members of each team begin the race by covering the distance with one tray each. They return and pass the trays to the next team members. Repeat until they have all completed their stint. The first team to finish wins. For smaller children, reduce the number of items and distance they have to travel. Repeat as time and enthusiasm permits. Finish with a leaders' race.

WIND UP 2

Review the questions from the Warm Up. Refer back to the game and the imprisonment of the baker and wine steward. Remind the children that, although it appeared hopeless for Joseph in prison, God was still with him and Joseph had not forgotten that. He reminded the baker and the wine steward that only God can make sense of dreams. So even in prison God was with Joseph. Is it going to get any better next week? The last thing we hear about Joseph is that his last chance was gone, the wine steward forgot about him and never gave him another thought. Will God come to his rescue?

JOSEPH GIVEN HIGH OFFICE

Text: Read and study Genesis 41:1-57.

Teaching Point: Joseph was positioned to save God's people from starvation.

WARM UP 1

A skit or puppets (see script on page 88). Toby is telling Trudy about an incident in the park. He was on his way to football training when he heard a cry for help. He followed the cries and found a little girl backed up by a tree with a big, fierce dog barking at her. Toby rescued the girl from the dog. Trudy is amazed at Toby's bravery. It turns out that the dog was not as big as Toby said and that it was only wanting to play. Toby kicked the football and the dog chased it. The little girl was full of gratitude and called Toby her saviour. Toby was in the right place at the right time.

Say, 'In today's true story from the Bible we will learn how God placed the right person in the right place to save his people and others from dying. Come back and tell me:

1. Who was the right person?
2. How did God put him where he wanted him?'

CONSOLIDATION 1

The object of the Consolidation is to demonstrate how difficult it can be to position the right person, with the right item in the right place at the right time. You will need:

- four different coloured hats (or numbered 1,2,3,4)
- four chairs numbered 1 - 4 or of different colours as above
- four different items such as a toothbrush, an umbrella, a soft toy, a newspaper or a book
- four volunteers, who are given a letter A, B, C, D.

The rest of the children act as the Mastermind. Ask the four volunteers to choose a hat and an item and sit down on a chair. Before the game begins, decide what is your preferred combination, e.g. Volunteer A should have a red hat, the toothbrush and sit on Chair number 3. There are many possible combinations.

Tell the Mastermind any correct choices that have been made, e.g. the right person in the right place, or the right person with the right hat, or the right person with the right item. If none of them are right, instruct the Mastermind to concentrate on one point at a time. First get the right person (A) into the right chair (3) by telling the organiser to rearrange the people onto different chairs. Once they have got A onto chair 3, (this could take a maximum of four turns), concentrate on getting the correct hat (red) onto A's head. Ask the Mastermind to move the hats around, one at a time, until the red one rests on person A. At the end of each change tell the Mastermind whether his combination is right or wrong. If time runs out, terminate the test by saying, 'Wasn't that hard?' If there are a large number of children divide them into teams and give each team a different combination to achieve. A leader acts as supervisor to give evaluations after each change.

WIND UP 1

Refer back to the Warm Up and review the questions with the children. Remind them of how difficult it was for the Mastermind to get the right person, with the right hat, on the right chair with the right item. It took lots and lots of tries to get it right and even then it may still have been wrong. God is not like us. He took Joseph out of prison and made him governor of Egypt, so that he could save God's people from the starvation to come. Ask the children to tell you every circumstance that brought Joseph to the right place so that he could be Governor of Egypt. God made the wine steward remember Joseph when it was important. God made it possible for Joseph to be in Egypt when the King had his disturbing dreams. God was always in control, organising the events for his purposes and his people. Joseph was God's person in God's place at God's time.

JOSEPH GIVEN HIGH OFFICE

Text: Read and study Genesis 41:1-57.

Teaching Point: Joseph was positioned to save God's people from starvation.

WARM UP 2

The object of the Warm Up is for the children to identify different ways a person can get out of prison. Pretend the area where the children are sitting is a prison and they have to suggest ways of getting out. Distinguish between acceptable ways of release, such as a pardon, and unacceptable ways, such as using violence to escape. Some suggestions could be visually displayed to arrest the children's attention, e.g.

- Piece of paper to represent a pardon
- A calendar to represent serving the full time of the sentence
- A metal saw to cut through the bars and escape
- A master key to open the doors and escape
- A rope to climb over the wall
- A ladder to climb over the wall and escape
- A helicopter to lift you out of the exercise yard
- A stick of TNT or plastic explosives to blow a hole in the wall
- Money to bribe your way out
- A gun / knife to force your way out
- A rubbish bin to hide in and escape with the dustman

When a child suggests a genuine way, write it down on a flip-chart or board and let them leave the prison area. Freedom is to one side of the main group. Continue while the suggestions are sensible. Some children will be left in prison because they cannot think of a different way from the ones already suggested. Their cause will look more hopeless as time passes. Will they ever get out?

Say, 'In today's true story from the Bible some one got out of prison without using any of the above methods. I want you to listen carefully to the Bible story and come back and tell me how God got his servant out of prison.'

CONSOLIDATION 2

The object of the game is for the children to escape from prison by means of an obstacle course. Divide the group into teams of equal numbers and ability. Each child needs a bag to place its shoes in. The obstacle course is simple but taxing. For each team stretch one 3-metre length of clothes-line in a straight line on the floor. Chalk or masking tape can be used instead. Place some chairs or a small table at the end of the clothes-line so that the children have to crawl under them.

Before the game starts ask the children to remove their shoes and put them in the bags to be carried to freedom, so that the prison guards won't hear them escaping. On the command, 'Go!' one child from each team walks along the clothes-line on the floor so that both feet are touching the line. When they get to the end they crawl under the chairs or table, at which time they have escaped. Then it is the turn of the next child to complete the course. The first team to finish wins. Replace the shoes once the game is concluded.

Explain that this was not the way God rescued Joseph. Not only did God get Joseph out of prison, but he also arranged for him to become Governor, the second most important man in Egypt.

WIND UP 2

Review the questions from the Warm Up, focusing on the unique way that God got Joseph out of prison and elevated him to the second most important position in Egypt. Freed and rewarded, God blessed Joseph wonderfully, so that he could save his people from starvation.

FAMILY RECONCILIATION

Text: Read and study Genesis 42:1 - 46:7.

Memory Verse: The Lord will hear when I call to him. Psalm 4:3

Teaching Point: To see the fulfilment of God's plan for Joseph.

WARM UP 1

The object of the Warm Up is to plan an event in detail, but not have it come to fulfilment. It will frustrate the children to have expectations that are not satisfied. Tell the children that you are going to have a party. You need their help in planning and preparing for it. Ask the children what sort of things you should have and either list them on a board or provide them from a secret box. Some suggestions are:

1. balloons (ask the older children and leaders to blow them up)
2. streamers (plait them into strands)
3. paper hats (you can make them out of newspaper)
4. noise makers, e.g. whistles
5. food and drink as appropriate
6. candles (but no matches)
7. table decorations (decorated cloth, napkins, serviettes, paper plates, cups)
8. cake
9. plastic bin liners for rubbish

Spend the rest of the time setting up as much of the party as you can. Make sure that it is obvious that the arrangements are incomplete. The children will want to continue, but that will defeat the whole purpose of the Warm Up.

Say, 'In today's true story from the Bible we will see the completion of God's plans for Joseph and his family. We couldn't complete our plans for the party, because we ran out of time, but we will see how God completed his plans for Joseph. Come back and tell me how he did it.'

CONSOLIDATION 1

Complete the preparation for the party, started in the Warm Up. Provide some light refreshments such as biscuits, crisps and fruit drink, to give it a party atmosphere. Prior to the lesson write the Bible memory verse on the underside of the paper plates to be used during the party. When everything has been consumed (which, like the locusts of Egypt, should not take long), ask the children to turn the plates over and read the verse together, 'The Lord will hear when I call to him. Psalm 4:3'. Remind the children of how that was demonstrated in Joseph's life.

WIND UP 1

This is the last lesson on Joseph and we can see how God made his plans come true to save his people (See Genesis 45: 5-9). Joseph was now happy to be friends with his brothers again, to see

his father and know that God was always controlling everything that happened. All the dreams of Joseph, the baker, the wine steward and the king came true, because they all were part of God's plan to save his people.

Lesson 17

FAMILY RECONCILIATION

Text: Read and study Genesis 42:1 - 46:7.

Teaching Point: To see the fulfilment of God's plan for Joseph.

WARM UP 2

The object of the Warm Up is to see if the children can find an object when it is hidden under a box or bucket. You need six kitchen buckets all of the same colour but opaque, a 'silver' cup, and five other objects that will fit under the buckets. (Ice cream containers or plastic beakers can be used instead of buckets and a silver cup can be made by wrapping kitchen foil around an egg cup.) Place the six kitchen buckets upside down on a table and place the five items and the silver cup on top of them. Go through the items one at a time, making sure the children know what they are. Place the items under the buckets so they cannot be seen. Ask the children if they can remember what was under a specific bucket? What about this one? Once you have established that the children know which item is under which bucket, move the buckets around. Do several changes to confuse the audience. Ask the children to tell you under which bucket a specific item is, not mentioning the silver cup. If the children get it right, they get a point. If they get it wrong the leader gets a point. Play the game as time allows and conclude by saying, 'The true story from the Bible today is about a hidden item and what happened to the person on whom it was found. I want you to come back and tell me:

1. What was the item?
2. In whose possession was it found?
3. What was supposed to happen to that person?
4. How did everything turn out?'

CONSOLIDATION 2

The object of the game is to avoid being caught with the bag containing the silver cup. Mark out a large safe area for the children to run around in. You will need six plastic shopping bags and six plastic cups. Place one disposable cup in each plastic bag and tie the handles together so that the cup cannot fall out. Give one bag to a child and tell them to hand it onto the child they tag. The tagged person takes the plastic bag and hands it to another child and the process repeats itself until the leader shouts, 'Stop!' The person holding the bag is out. Repeat until only one is left. When a winner is found, declare all the children who are out, 'Forgiven', and recommence the game as time, energy and enthusiasm permits.

To make the game more interesting you can add the other five bags one at a time, so that several children are attempting to tag people.

WIND UP 2

Review the questions from the Warm Up. Summarise the final chapter in the story of Joseph, i.e. how he was reconciled and reunited with his father and brothers and how he saved God's people from the famine.

Tell the children that, in spite of his brothers hating him and trying to kill him, in spite of him being sold into slavery, in spite of being put in prison when innocent, in spite of being forgotten by his friends, in spite of all the bad things that happened to Joseph, God brought good out of it by making him Governor of Egypt. In this way God honoured his covenant promise to his people and saved them from starvation.

GOD PROVIDES A DELIVERER

Text: Read and study Exodus 1:1 - 2:10

Memory verse: In all things God works for good. Romans 8:28

Teaching Point: To teach that God is in control

WARM UP 1

Discuss what it means to be 'in charge' - responsible for sorting out any problems as well as telling people what to do. Start with who is in charge at school. Let the children point out who is in charge and tell you why. Move on to who is in charge on the football pitch. Next, point the children to a map of their own country. Ask them the name of the country and who is in charge. (Try to get a map that is brightly coloured but not complicated.) Lastly, display a model or picture of the stars, universe and solar system. Ask who is in charge of all. Say, 'In today's true story from the Bible we will find out whether God is also in control of events and circumstances.' Send the children off to Bible time with the following questions:

1. What was happening to God's people?
2. Why was it happening?
3. What was the name of the baby?

CONSOLIDATION 1

The object of the game is to reinforce the story details. Divide the group into multi-age teams of not more than eight children, each team with a leader. Prepare one set of memory verse words per team by writing one word of the Bible verse, including the reference, onto each piece of card or paper. Place the shuffled memory verse cards in piles at the opposite end of the room from the teams and give each team leader a set of eight questions and answers from the Bible passage. The questions should be age specific, so that a younger child is asked an easier question than an older child. The leader reads out the questions one at a time.

As each question is asked, the child who answers correctly runs to the other end of the room, collects one word of the memory verse and brings it back to base. The winner is the first team to collect all eight cards and put them in the correct order.

GOD PROVIDES A DELIVERER

Text: Read and study Exodus 1:1 - 2:10

Memory verse: In all things God works for good. Romans 8:28.

Teaching Point: To teach that God is in control

WIND UP 1

Talk about who is in control, i.e. God. How did God show he was in control? Go over the answers to the Warm Up questions. Point out how God saved Moses and arranged for him to grow up in the King's palace. Revise the memory verse.

WARM UP 2

Prepare a box containing a collection of items, some to do with the story and some not. Suggested items are a baby doll, a basket, picture of a river, crown, jacket, picture of a mountain, toy solider, etc. Show the children the items one at a time, each time asking, 'Do you think this is in today's Bible story?' Separate the items depending on the children's answers. After all items have been displayed, allow the children the opportunity to change their minds. Tell them to come back after the story and see if they are right. Send them off to Bible time with the following questions:

1. What was happening to God's people?
2. Why was it happening?
3. What was the name of the baby?

CONSOLIDATION 2

Play a finding game. Divide the children into small groups of two or three, with a leader or older child in charge. Prepare a series of cards for each group, using the cradle or Moses basket template below. The sets can either be the eight words of the memory verse, including reference, or a series of eight pictures telling the story. Each word or picture in the set should be a different colour, i.e. you need eight different colours. Hide the cradles around the room. The children have to find one of each colour cradles, then place them in the correct order.

WIND UP 2

Go through the items from the Warm Up, using them to pick up on the story details. Go over the answers to the Warm Up questions. Remind them of the Bible verse, using the cradles. Repeat/ learn the Bible verse.

GOD PREPARES A DELIVERER

Text: Read and study Exodus 3:1 - 4:17

Teaching Point: To show how God equips his servant for the job that he is given to do.

WARM UP 1

Select someone to run the Sunday School. Explain that they must be able to tell the Bible story. Pick a candidate from the big children or leaders. Ask the children if they would choose this one. Ask for volunteers from the audience. Continue until a pre-identified person is selected. He offers excuses why he cannot tell the Bible story. Choose three from the following:

- Nobody can understand his accent
- Nobody would listen
- He is too shy
- He has big feet
- He hasn't been trained properly
- He can't remember things.

Encourage him to try anyway and explain how to overcome his seeming difficulties.

- To overcome the accent, speak slowly
- Have children promise to listen
- The children are his friends
- Children might not notice the feet
- I will train him as he goes on
- I will give him clues as he goes along

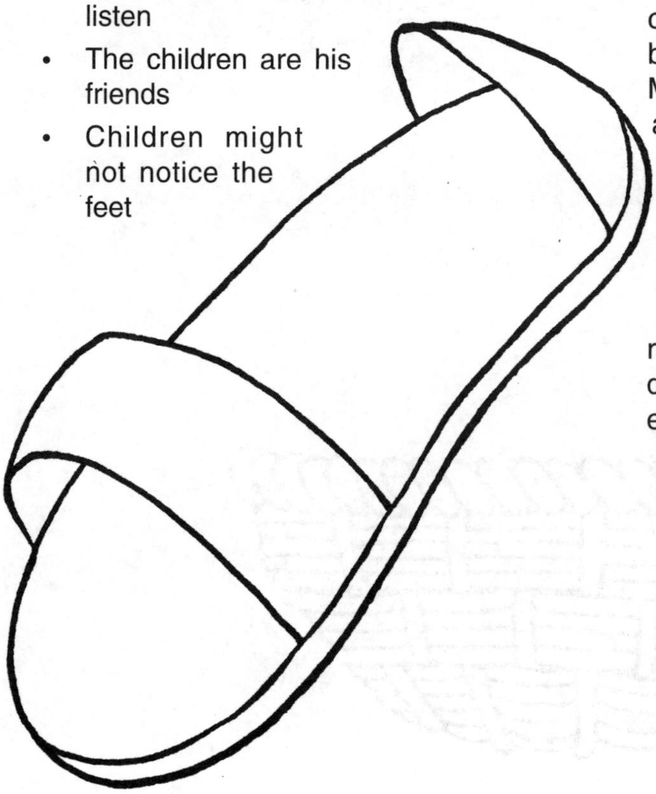

Ask the new leader to review last week's story.

Send the children off to Bible time with the following questions:

1. What was the name of the man God chose?
2. Did the man think he was the right person for the job?
3. How did God show him that he was the right person?

CONSOLIDATION 1

Prepare one piece of A4 paper per child, cut out in the shape of a sandal (see template). The sandals should be in a variety of colours. Scatter the sandals over the floor. Prepare an area with a leader in charge to be the 'Sin Bin'. The children move around to music. When the music stops each child stands on a sandal. Designate all the children on a certain colour sandal as out, because they did not take off their sandals like Moses did at the burning bush. The children who are out go to the 'Sin Bin' for one turn. Choose a different colour sandal to be out each time.

WIND UP 1

Go over the answers to the Warm Up questions. Remind the children that God is holy, referring to the game. God knew what he was doing when he appointed Moses. Go over Moses' excuses and how God dealt with each one.

GOD PREPARES A DELIVERER

Text: Read and study Exodus 3:1 - 4:17

Teaching Point: To show how God equips his servant for the job that he is given to do.

WARM UP 2

Choosing the right person for the job. Prepare a series of pictures, matching up the person with the job. Suggested pairs:

doctor	sick person
lollipop lady	busy road with child
fireman	fire
garage man	broken down car
postman	letters
plumber	leaking tap
teacher	classroom

Pin up the pictures of the jobs on one side of the board and the people on the other. Point to the job, asking, 'Which of these people is the right person to do this job?' Play around, asking if the children are sure. Point out that all the jobs have to be done by people who have been trained to do them. Say, 'In today's true story from the Bible we will find out how God chose someone to do an important job.' Send the children off to Bible time with the following questions:

1 What is the name of the man God chose?

2 Did the man think he was the right person?

3 How did God show him that he was the right person?

CONSOLIDATION 2

The children line up down the centre of the room with the leader at the head. Explain that they are slaves, under your command. Designate three areas of the room - pyramids, fields, and work. Go over the responses to the various commands.

Go to bed	lie down
Collect straw	bend down and pick up
Make bricks	squat
Go to the pyramids	move to pyramids area
Go to work	move to work area
Return home	come back to line
Go to the fields	move to fields area
Salute the King	salute
Pray to God	on knees
Climb the wall	climbing action

Call out the commands in random order. Children who get the command wrong miss one turn.

WIND UP 2

God's people were slaves, like in the game. God knew they needed rescuing. Remind them of the Warm Up - the importance of choosing the right person. Whom did God choose? God knew Moses was the right person for the job, even though Moses didn't think he was. God never makes mistakes.

GOD DEMONSTRATES HIS POWER

Text: Read and study Exodus 5:1 - 10:29.

Teaching point: To teach that God's plan cannot be thwarted.

WARM UP 1

Play 'Who wants to win a ...?' (choose a prize). The leader is the quizmaster. Beforehand scatter a selection of small sweets on a table at the back of the room. You need at least one sweet per child. Mark one sweet and give it to a child who has been primed what to do. Send all the children to pick a sweet and return to the front. Ask which child has the sweet with the mark. That one has been chosen to play, 'Who wants to win a ...?'

Prepare four questions from the preceding lesson, each question having four possible answers, three wrong and one right. Tell the children that the player has to answer four questions correctly to win the prize. If the player does not know the answer he has two lives; he can go 50/50 and he can ask the audience. The 50/50 card means that two wrong answers will be removed, leaving the right answer and 1 wrong answer. As each question is asked, display the question and the four possible answers, on a board or OHP. The player answers the first threequestions correctly. When the fourth question is asked the player does not know the answer. First, he uses the 50/50 card. He still does not know the answer so he asks the audience. The audience votes by putting up their hands. The audience should give the right answer. The player decides he knows better than the audience and gives the wrong answer, so he goes home with nothing.

Say, 'In today's true story from the Bible we will find out what happened when someone did not make the right decision, even when his advisors told him what the right thing was.' Send the children off to Bible time with the following questions:

1. Who was the man?
2. What decision did he have to make?
3. Who were his advisors?

CONSOLIDATION 1

Use the mnemonic, **B**est **F**ootball **G**ame **F**or **A**ges **B**ut **H**ugh **L**et **D**ick **D**ribble, to teach the order of the plagues. Go through the mnemonic with the children before the game starts. Divide the children into teams of no more than 10 people. Each team requires one set of cards containing one word of the mnemonic on each card and a picture of the plague on the back. Each team member has to negotiate an obstacle course (see below), pick up a card and return to base. The first person must return to base before the next person goes. The first team to collect their cards and place the mnemonic in the correct order wins.

Obstacle course: from home base, negotiate a set of stepping stones (to cross the River Nile), then jump like a frog as far as a table. Crawl under the table (to hide from the slave master) and run to the collection point, pick up a card and run home.

WIND UP 1

Review the questions from the Warm Up. Go over the order of the plagues, using the mnemonic cards. Point out how silly Pharaoh was not to listen to his advisers, just like the person behaved in the Warm Up. Remind them that God's words always come true - his plan cannot be thwarted.

GOD DEMONSTRATES HIS POWER

Text: Read and study Exodus 5:1 - 10:29.

Teaching point: To teach that God's plan cannot be thwarted.

WARM UP 2

Puppets or a skit (see script on page 89). Trudy tells Toby that their schoolteacher has said that they must perform a specified task by the next day. Toby does not believe her and goes out with his friends. The next day after school Trudy is busy at home and Toby arrives late. He had to stay late, because he did not complete the set task. As a result, he missed out on taking part in a football match. Toby is very unhappy.

Say, 'In today's true story from the Bible God sends a message to someone, who doesn't believe it. I want you to come back and tell me:

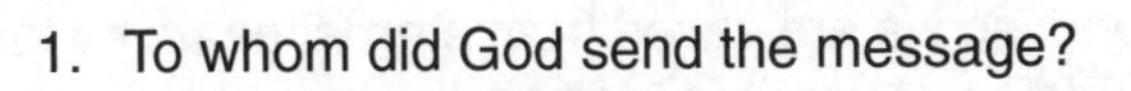

1. To whom did God send the message?
2. What was the message?
3. What did God do about it when the man didn't believe him?'

CONSOLIDATION 2

Prepare a bag of cards, each one containing either a plague or a decoy, e.g. a cake. Designate nine areas and pin up a picture of one of the first nine plagues at each place. The children move around to music. When the music stops, the leader picks a card out of the bag and calls out what is on it. If a plague is called out, the children run to the appropriate base. If a decoy is called out, they stay where they are. The last children to reach an area can be eliminated if wished.

WIND UP 2

Review the questions from the Warm Up. Pharaoh didn't believe God. What happened? Go over the order of plagues. Point out that Pharaoh was a powerful king, but he could not prevent God's words coming true. God's plans can never be thwarted.

GOD DELIVERS HIS PEOPLE

Text: Read and study Exodus 11:1 - 12:42.

Teaching Point: The importance of obeying God's instructions.

WARM UP 1

This Warm Up highlights obedience. Tell the children they are in the army, so have to obey their commanding officer. Perform various actions, e.g. stand to attention, stand at ease, star jumps, cycling in the air, hopping, etc. Get them to stand in line and inspect the troops. Then march round the room in line. Say, 'In today's true story from the Bible God's people were given some instructions they had to obey.

1. What was God's plan for his people?
2. What instructions did God give them?
3. What was the result?'

CONSOLIDATION 1

The object is to demonstrate the importance of following instructions. The children are given instructions to follow to collect eight items to do with God's instructions to his people. The items are pictures of a lamb, a bowl and hyssop, a doorframe, bitter herbs, unleavened bread, a cloak, sandals and a staff. On the back of each picture is a letter -

P A S S O V E R.

Divide the children into families consisting of one leader (or older child) and a small group of children. Designate eight locations and place a different item at each location. You need the same number of each item as there are families. Each family has a list of eight questions and answers about the Bible story with instructions to follow. The leader asks his family the questions. When he gets the answer he follows the instruction attached to that question, e.g. go to the big table and collect one item. The letters are collected in random order, then placed in the order of the story. Turn the pictures over to see if the order is correct. (When in correct order the letters on the back spell 'Passover'.)

It is preferable if each family collects from locations in a different order,

e.g.

team A:	1	3	5	7	2	4	6	8
team B:	2	4	6	8	3	5	7	1
team C:	3	5	7	1	4	6	8	2
team D:	4	6	8	2	5	7	1	3

WIND UP 1

Review the questions from the Warm Up. Talk about God's plan for his people. Was it important that his people obeyed God's instructions? Link to the game. They needed to obey instructions in order to get the right word at the end. Point out that the Passover is a picture of the cross. In the same way that the firstborn were saved from physical death by the shedding of the lamb's blood, so we are saved from eternal death by the shedding of Jesus' blood on the cross.

GOD DELIVERS HIS PEOPLE

Text: Read and study Exodus 11:1 - 12:42.

Teaching Point: To show how God saves his people from death and slavery in Egypt.

WARM UP 2

If you have a convenient door frame cover it with masking tape and daub it with red paint, using a bunch of foliage. Otherwise make a doorframe from card and set it up in the teaching area. The children can pass through it to go for their Bible story.

Start by reminding the children of where you have got to in the story of the rescue of God's people from Egypt. Say, 'There was one last thing that God was going to do to make the Egyptians let his people go. Watch carefully, because what I do next is part of the story.' Paint the doorframe. Send the children to Bible time with the following questions:

1. What did the people use to paint their doorways?
2. Why did they have to do it?

An alternative to the above is to provide a selection of things to paint, such as pieces of paper and card, hard boiled eggs, etc. along with different painting implements. These can be different sized brushes as well as pieces of rag, your fingers, etc. Ask the children to tell you which implement to use to paint the different items on display.

Say, 'In today's true story from the Bible we will see how God told his people to paint something. I want you to come back and tell me:

1. What did the people have to paint?
2. What did they use?
3. Why did they have to do this?'

CONSOLIDATION 2

Divide the children into teams. Place one child from each team on a chair (island) with a series of stepping stones leading to it. Tell the children that the child on the island needs rescuing and each team must designate one team member to be the rescuer. The rescuer can only move from stepping stone to stepping stone if the remaining team members answer the question correctly. The questions are on the preceding three lessons. You need two more questions than the number of stepping stones. Each team needs a leader or older child to ask the questions and tell the rescuer when he can move. Once the rescuer arrives at the chair the child is safe.

WIND UP 2

Remind the children of the painting activity. Review the questions from the Warm Up. Did the people follow God's instructions? Were they rescued? Link back to the game.

GOD DESTROYS HIS ENEMIES

Text: Read and study Exodus 13:17 – 14:31

Teaching Point: To show how God saved his people from destruction.

WARM UP 1

Produce something precious and show it to the children. While this is going on another leader comes in and wants to take the precious item and destroy it. Leader 1 tries reasoning with Leader 2, but to no avail. Then Leader 1 sends Leader 2 away, but Leader 2 returns. Eventually the only option left is to call the police (Leader 3), who takes Leader 2 off to gaol. Explain that sometimes someone is determined to destroy something that is precious and the only way you can stop them doing it is to remove them from the situation. Say, 'In today's true story from the Bible we will find out what happened when someone wanted to destroy something that was precious to God. Come back and tell me:

1. Who was precious to God?
2. Who was determined to destroy the precious thing?
3. How was the destroyer removed?'

CONSOLIDATION 1

This Consolidation consists of two short games.

Game 1 - Divide the children into two equal groups. Form them into two lines facing each other. The children lie down flat with their feet touching the feet of their opposite number. The leader walks through the middle of the two lines of children. As he goes, the children quickly raise their legs to the vertical to give the impression of the sea parting. Rehearse the children so that no one touches the leader as he walks through. When the children understand the game the leader will start with the words, 'Red Sea', at which the first two children will raise their legs like drawbridges. Repeat the process with the leader moving faster and faster as the game progresses. Safety is always paramount. The children can shout, 'Red Sea' when the leader gets to them and they raise their legs. At the end ask the children:

1. Why was the Red Sea parted?
2. How was the Red Sea parted?
3. Did everyone reach the other side safely? (Remember that the Egyptians were drowned.)

Game 2 - Leaders hold up a sheet or parachute. The children run underneath from one side to the other, then around the outside to their starting point and repeat. On the call of 'Israelites', the sheet is raised; on the call of 'Egyptians', the sheet is lowered, trapping those underneath. Children who are caught are sent to the 'Sin Bin' and miss one turn.

WIND UP 1

Review the questions from the Warm Up. Use the games to remind the children of the details of the story. Point out that the Israelites were God's precious possession and he had promised to rescue them. Because the Egyptians would not let the Israelites go, God had to destroy them.

GOD DESTROYS HIS ENEMIES

Text: Read and study Exodus 13:17 – 14:31

Teaching Point: To show how God saved his people from destruction.

WARM UP 2

A skit or puppets (see script on page 90). Toby and Trudy are very excited because Aunt Mary is due to take them to the zoo. Toby points out that Aunt Mary has not arrived yet, so how do they know she will come? Trudy reminds him that Aunt Mary wrote to their parents to say she would come today to take them to the zoo. Toby says that people do not always do what they say they will, and recounts the story of what happened when he took his pet mouse to school. George had promised him a bar of chocolate if he let the mouse loose in the classroom. When he did so he got a detention from the teacher and George did not give him the bar of chocolate. Trudy says that grown-ups are different, but Toby is not convinced. Toby goes off, because he does not believe Aunt Mary will come. Trudy is left wondering what to do. Aunt Mary has always kept her promises before, but she is late.

The leader comments on Trudy's dilemma. Should she do what Aunt Mary said? Why? Leader says, 'In today's true story from the Bible, God's people were in a difficult situation. God told them what to do to escape. I want you to come back and tell me:

1. What was the difficult situation?
2. Why were they there?
3. How did God rescue his people from the difficult situation?
4. (For older children) What did God's people do when they saw the great power God displayed against the Egyptians?'

CONSOLIDATION 2

The object is to see who can be the first to get their equipment across the Red Sea. Divide the children into two teams - cloud and fire. Each team requires a selection of transportable items of different sizes, at least two items per child. Pile the items at one end of the room and pin up a picture of a pillar of fire and one of a pillar of cloud at the other end. The children take the items one at a time and run with them across the sea to the other end. To make the game more taxing, the sea can be crossed by a line of stepping stones, e.g. mats. Once the child has deposited the item by their pillar they must run back and tag the next child in the line. Once all the items have been carried over the sea the children run across one at a time. The winner is the first team to get all their equipment and people to the other side.

WIND UP 2

Remind the children of Trudy's dilemma and review the questions from the Warm Up. Did the Israelites trust God and do what he said. Link to the game. Point out that God had promised to rescue the Israelites. Because the Egyptians would not let the Israelites go, God had to destroy them. God always keeps his promises.

GOD GIVES FOOD

Text: Read and study Exodus 16:1-36.

Teaching point: To see how God provided for his people's material needs.

WARM UP 1

Prepare a box of different food and non-food items, either real or pictures. Ask the children, 'What do we eat?' Bring the items out of the box one at a time. Is this good to eat? If the answer is yes, put on the table marked with a tick, if no, put on the table marked with a cross. If using pictures, pin on a board under the tick or cross as appropriate. Once all the items are displayed, review the food items one at a time. What would happen if this one were not available? Remove that item and replace in the box. Continue until all the items are gone.

Say, 'In today's true story from the Bible God's people had run out of food. There were no shops to go to. I want you to come back and tell me:

1. Did the people trust God to sort out the problem?
2. How did God look after his people?'

CONSOLIDATION 1

The object is to gather 'manna' and discover that each person gets the same reward, regardless of how much manna has been gathered, thus reinforcing some of the story details. The manna can be lentils, small scraps of paper or table tennis balls. Scatter the manna over the area. Divide the children in to 'family' groups and give each group a container to collect their manna. At the end of the game, each family group takes what they have gathered to the leader, who changes their manna for a food reward, such as a biscuit or small piece of bread for each family member. Each group gets the same reward, regardless of how much they gathered.

WIND UP 1

Point out that God knew his people needed food. Review the questions from the Warm Up. Remind the children that when the Israelites gathered the manna and weighed it they all had the same amount. Link back to the game.

GOD GIVES FOOD

Text: Read and study Exodus 16:1-36.

Teaching point: To see how God provided for his people's material needs.

WARM UP 2

The object is to demonstrate the importance of trusting the leader. Ask the children, 'Do you trust me?' Blindfold some volunteers and tell them you are going to give them something to eat. Do they trust you to give them good things? One at a time ask the volunteers to hold out their hands and place a piece of food on them. The food should feel unpleasant, e.g. a peeled grape, a piece of mango, a piece of banana. If they trust you they will eat it. Ask them to open their mouths so that you can pop a piece of food in. Use a piece of biscuit or bread. If they trust you they will do it.

Say, 'In today's true story from the Bible God's people had a problem. Did they trust God to sort it out? I want you to come back and tell me:

1. What was the problem?
2. Did the people immediately trust God to sort it out? (no, they grumbled)
3. How did God sort it out?'

CONSOLIDATION 2

The object is to have some fun, using some of the detail from the story. Divide the children into teams. Each team requires one 'quail' made from a table tennis ball coloured brown. Divide the team in two and place half at each end of the room. The team members take it in turns to roll, using their noses, the quail from one end of the room to the other. Keep going until each team member has changed places and the quail is finally caught.

WIND UP 2

Do we trust God? Link back to the Warm Up. Did the volunteers trust the leader to give them good things to eat? Review the questions from the Warm Up. What food did God provide? We have been having fun chasing quails. It would not have been so much fun for the Israelites! Could the Israelites trust God to provide for their daily need of food? Can we trust God to provide for our needs too? If your children know the Lord's Prayer, this would be a good way to finish.

GOD GIVES WATER AND VICTORY

Text: Read and study Exodus 17:1-16.

Memory verse: God will supply all your needs. Philippians 4 verse 19

Teaching Point: To see how God provided for his people's need for water and victory.

WARM UP 1

What do we need to live happily? Prior to the lesson pin up pictures face down of things we need to live happily, e.g. food, drink, toys, a house, parents/family, friends, money, clothes, etc. (The pictures should be identified on the back so that you know which one to turn over.) Include some spare sheets of plain paper to record any suggestions that are not covered by the pictures. Ask the children to make suggestions and turn over the appropriate picture or record it on a plain sheet of paper. Ask the children whom they ask if they want some more food, drink, clothes, etc. *(parents)*. Remind the children of last week's lesson - what did the people need and who provided for their need?

Say, 'In today's true story from the Bible we will hear what happened to God's people next. The Israelites are in trouble in the desert.' Send the children off to class with the following questions:

1. What were the two problems?
2. How did they get out of trouble?
3. What did they forget? *(God's power and previous care)*

CONSOLIDATION 1

A team game designed to revise the story and memory verse. Each team should be no bigger than 10 children. Prepare one set of memory verse words per team. Each set must be on a different coloured paper. Prepare one set of 10 questions about the Bible story for each team. Divide the children into multi-age teams. The leader reads out the first question and addresses it to a specific age group. This allows the younger children to be involved. The child who answers correctly runs to the end of the room to collect one word of the memory verse and bring it back to base. Continue until all the questions have been answered. The winner is the first team to collect the memory verse words and put them in the correct order.

WIND UP 1

Review the Warm Up questions prior to the game. After the game remind the children of the Warm Up - what we need to live a happy life. Who provides those needs? What did God provide for his people last week? What did God provide this week? How does God provide for our needs? Repeat the memory verse.

GOD GIVES WATER AND VICTORY

Text: Read and study Exodus 17:1-16.

Teaching Point: To see how God provided for his people's need for water and victory.

WARM UP 2

Show the children a glass of clear water. Would anyone like a drink? Then show them a glass of water discoloured with food colouring. Would anyone like a drink of that? Have a discussion about being thirsty. Have you ever been really, really thirsty? How does it feel? Talk about how long a person can go without water compared with food (only a few days), as this underlines the predicament. What can you do about it? Who do you ask for help? Why do you ask that person? *(Because they've always helped in the past.)*

Say, 'In today's true story from the Bible we will find out what happened when God's people were really, really thirsty.

I want you to come back and tell me:

1. Did they ask for help?
2. How did God provide for them?
3. What else happened to show them that God was looking after them?'

CONSOLIDATION 2

This game is a mix of musical statues and following instructions. The children move around to music. When the music stops, the children freeze. Then the leader gives an instruction, e.g. run away (to side of room). If the leader has his hands up in the air the children obey. If he has his hands down the children stay where they are (or fall down dead). Suggested instructions are: run away, draw your sword, jump up and down, hop on one leg, form groups of two (or three), stand to attention, etc. Ensure that the children understand the various instructions they might be given. It is helpful to have a rehearsal run through first.

WIND UP 2

Review the questions from the Warm Up. Remind the children of the battle. Link back to the game. When Moses held his hands up the Israelites prevailed. When he held his hands down the enemy prevailed.

Lesson 25

GOD GIVES INSTRUCTIONS

Text: Read and study Exodus 19:1 - 20:21; 31:18

Teaching Point: God gave rules for the benefit of his people.

WARM UP 1

Have a selection of nice foods, such as cornflakes, baked beans, drinking chocolate, etc. Ask, 'Who likes eating cornflakes?' A volunteer has a few. Repeat the question for each of the foods, allowing a different volunteer to sample each one. Then mix them up together. Who likes eating this? A leader volunteers and tries one mouthful. It is disgusting. Point out to the children that we have rules about which foods go together. When we ignore those rules we end up with something that is not nice.

Say, 'In today's true story from the Bible we see what happened when God gave his people some rules about the way that they should behave. I want you to come back and tell me:

1. Where were the people when this happened?
2. What was the name of the man whom God gave the rules to?
3. Why weren't all the people present?'

CONSOLIDATION 1

The object is to see what happens when people do not follow instructions. Give children various instructions to follow. Secretly instruct a leader to do the opposite of the commands. Examples of instructions are:

• Run from one end of the room to the other with no body contact.

• Roll from one end of the room to the other with no body contact.

• Carry a collection of items from one end of the room to another without dropping any.

• Disposable cups are a minefield. Walk from one end of the room to the other without touching the cups.

WIND UP

Review the questions from the Warm Up. Remind the children that ignoring the food rules resulted in nasty things to eat. Breaking the rules of the game spoiled it for everyone. Why did God give his people rules? So that they could live happily with God and with each other.

GOD GIVES INSTRUCTIONS

Text: Read and study Exodus 19:1 - 20:21; 31:18

Teaching Point: God gave rules for the benefit of his people.

WARM UP 2

Show the children pictures of different road signs and ask them to identify them. Start the children at one end of the room and ask them to walk towards you. Use some of the road signs as flash cards. When you hold them up the children have to obey them. Signs you could use are: stop, turn right, slow, etc. Discuss why we need them. What happens if we disobey them? Point out that the rules of the road are for our benefit. They allow us to get to our destination safely.

Say, 'In today's true story from the Bible we will see what happened when God gave his people instructions. I want you to come back and tell me:

1. Where did God give the Israelites his instructions?
2. What was the name of the man to whom God gave the instructions?
3. Why wasn't everyone there?'

CONSOLIDATION 2

The object is to demonstrate the consequences of not following instructions. Mark off an area to be the 'Sin Bin'. The home base is in the centre of the room. (This could be a sheet that everyone has to get under.) Mark four compass points at the edge of the room with the letters N, S, E and W. The children start at the home base. The leader shouts out a compass point and the children run to it. Those who go to the wrong point are out and go to the 'Sin Bin'. Continue until only one child is left. Alternatively, when out the children miss two turns in the 'Sin Bin', then rejoin the game.

WIND UP 2

Remind the children of the need for road signs. Review the questions from the Warm Up. Refer back to the game and the consequences of not following instructions. Remind the children that God gave his people instructions to follow so that they could live happily with him and with each other.

ABOUT PUTTING GOD FIRST

Text: Read and study Exodus 20:3, Joshua 24:1-24.

Teaching Point: One day we must decide whether or not we will serve God.

WARM UP 1

Set up a restaurant with three tables. You need one leader to be the waiter and three leaders to be customers, each at a different table. Leader 1 calls the waiter and makes an order. Then Leader 2 calls the waiter over and demands something. The waiter deliberates aloud, 'What should I do first?' Then Leader 3 demands something. The waiter is in a real state, wondering whom to serve first. Eventually he decides to serve Leader 1 first, as he was the first to order.

Say, 'In today's true story from the Bible we will learn about some people who had to make a decision. I want you to come back and tell me:

1. Who were the people?
2. What was the name of their leader?
3. What decision did they have to make?'

CONSOLIDATION 1

Place sheets or parachutes in four corners of the room. The children stand in the centre. The leader calls out, 'Choose', and the children run to one of the sheets and get under it. One group is declared out. Repeat, making different corners out in random order. The children have to move to a different parachute each time

WIND UP 1

Review the questions from the Warm Up. Point out the importance of God's people making the right choice to follow God. Link in to the game and the results of them making the wrong choice. Explain simply that one day we all will have to make the same choice as God's people in the Bible story - whether or not we will be God's friends and serve him. Point out that the choice to follow God is not random, like choosing which corner to go to in the game, but obvious. God tells us all that we need to know in order to follow him; our job is to obey his word. Do **not** put any pressure on the children to make a decision there and then.

ABOUT PUTTING GOD FIRST

Text: Read and study Exodus 20:3, Joshua 24:1-24.

Teaching Point: One day we must decide whether or not we will serve God.

WARM UP 2

Use the game show format, 'Play Your Cards Right'. Either use large playing cards, or make your own with numbers written on them. Divide the children down the middle into two teams. Each team requires nine cards stuck in a row on a board face down. Decide which team goes first, e.g. ask one of the team members to give you a number between 3 and 5. If they get it right their team starts. Turn over the first card in the row. The team has to decide whether the next card in the row is higher or lower. (Ace plays high if using playing cards.) The whole team has to agree and they show their choice by standing up for higher and remaining sitting for lower. (For older children you could use thumbs up for higher and thumbs down for lower.) The team carries on making choices for as long as they are right. Once they make a wrong choice the game moves to the other team. Continue until both teams have turned over all their cards. When preparing the cards make sure that the order is such that there will be some surprising results, e.g. a 3 followed by a 2, or a 10 followed by a Jack or 11.

Say, 'In today's true story from the Bible we will learn about some people who had to make an important choice. I want you to come back and tell me:

1. Who were the people?
2. What was the name of their leader?
3. What choice did they have to make?'

CONSOLIDATION 2

Place four leaders or older children in the corners of the room. The remaining children remain in the centre. The four leaders call to the children to come to them. The children choose which leader to go to. The children line up behind their leader and follow him around the room, performing various actions instituted by the leader. One group is declared out because they followed the wrong leader. The remaining children return to the centre and the game is repeated with all the leaders calling again. Leaders are declared 'wrong' in random order. Either repeat until only a few children are left, or just have the children miss one turn and then return to the game.

WIND UP 2

Review the questions from the Warm Up. Point out the importance of God's people making the right choice to follow God. Link in to the game and the results of them making the wrong choice. Whom we choose to follow is important and has consequences. Explain simply that one day we all will have to make the same choice as God's people in the Bible story - whether or not we will be God's friends and serve him. We know who is the right person to follow, unlike the game. Do **not** put any pressure on the children to make a decision there and then.

HOLY BIBLE

ABOUT SERVING GOD ONLY

Text: Read and study Exodus 20:4-6; 32:1-35.

Teaching Point: An idol is anything that is more important than God.

WARM UP 1

Either use puppets or act out a skit about the result of disobedience. (See page 91) The characters are two children, Child 1 tends to be disobedient and Child 2 is a goody-goody. Child 1 enters, looking for Child 2, because he has something important to tell her. Child 2 comes in, having been interrupted doing homework. Child 1 cannot be bothered with homework, even though he knows he will get into trouble if it is not done by the next day, but would rather try out his new roller blades. Child 2 reminds Child 1 that dad said he must wear pads and a helmet. Child 1 does not want to wear them, because they look sissy. He does not want to do what Dad tells him, because he thinks he knows best. Child 1 exits, followed by a loud noise. Child 2 dashes off to see what has happened, then returns to say that Child 1 has fallen and hit his head, so is being taken to hospital.

In today's true story from the Bible we will learn about a time when God's people disobeyed one of his commandments/instructions/rules. Ask the children to listen carefully so that they can tell you:

1. Which commandment did the people disobey?
2. How did they disobey it?
3. What was the result?

CONSOLIDATION 1

The 'No Idols Game'. Place a partition across the centre of the area and divide the group into two teams, one on each side of the partition. Give each group an equal number of soft objects that can be thrown over the partition, e.g. sponges or balls of scrunched up newspaper. Inform the children that each team is in its house and the sponges are idols. The idol police are coming round to see if they have any idols, so they must get rid of as many as possible. The aim of the game is to throw the idols over the partition into the other team's house. Periodically, stop the game to count the idols to see who is winning. At the end of the game the team with the least idols wins.

WIND UP 1

Remind the children of the consequences of Child 1 disobeying his parents' rules. Review the questions from the Warm Up. Link into the game and the importance of getting rid of anything that is more important than God. Review the second commandment. Remind the children that God gives us rules for our benefit.

ABOUT SERVING GOD ONLY

Text: Read and study Exodus 20:4-6; 32:1-35.

Teaching Point: An idol is anything that is more important than God.

WARM UP 2

Say to the children, 'I really miss my mum. I don't see her often, but I've got this to remind me of her.' Bring out a toy mouse, rubber chicken, etc. 'Every time I look at this it reminds me of my mum. I used to carry it round with me so I could be reminded of my mum. Now I've put it on the mantelpiece at home. When I speak to mum on the phone, I look at the chicken and it reminds me of who I'm talking to. In fact, I don't really need to phone mum at all, because I can talk to the chicken. In fact, I often find myself talking to the chicken. Mum phoned the other day and asked if she could come to stay, but it wasn't convenient, so I said no. After all, why do I need mum when I have this rubber chicken?'

Point out how silly it would be to have a rubber chicken instead of your mum. In today's true story from the Bible we learn about a time when God's people were silly. Ask the children to listen carefully so that they can tell you:

1. Which commandment did the people disobey?
2. How did they disobey it?
3. What was the result?

CONSOLIDATION 2

The object is to show how easy it is to go the wrong way. Make a tunnel with two exits (see diagram). Station a leader at each exit with coloured tokens, a different colour for each exit. Each child goes through and comes out of one of the exits, collecting a coloured token from the leader.

If there are lots of children and space permits, you may need more than one tunnel. Otherwise send the children through in pairs. Once all the children have been through the tunnel divide them into two groups depending on the colour of their token. Then tell them which token was the right choice.

WIND UP 2

Refer to the Warm Up, commenting on the stupidity of having a rubber chicken instead of your mum. Review the questions from the Warm Up. Link back to the game and the consequences of making the wrong choice. Point out that, unlike the game, God does not leave us in the dark regarding choosing to put him first.

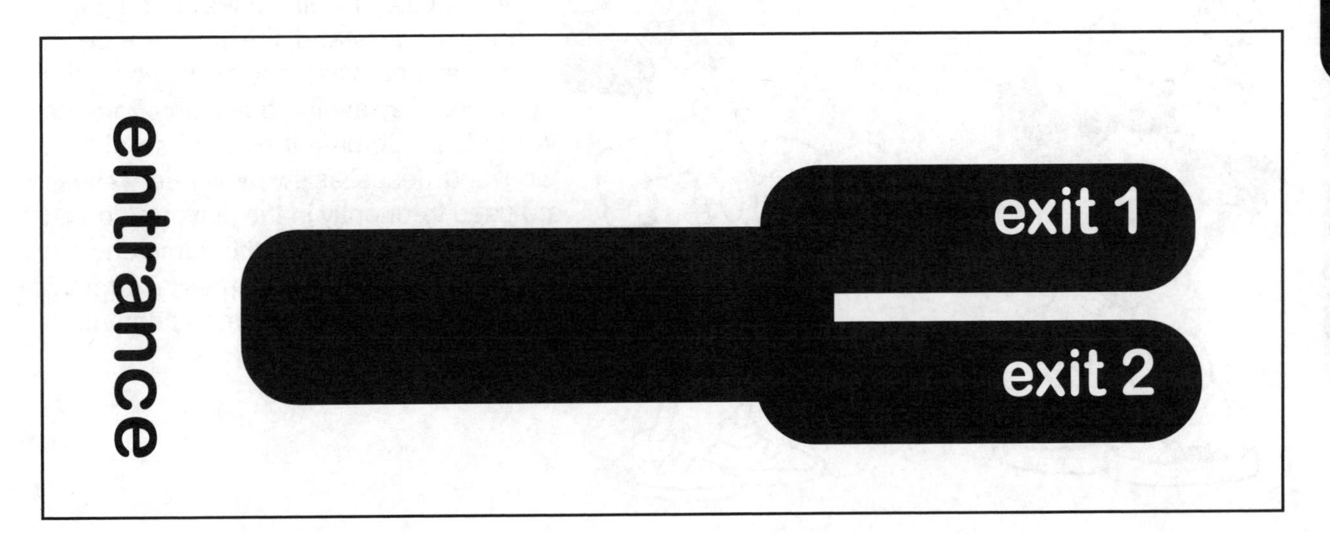

ABOUT THE USE OF GOD'S NAME

Text: Read and study Exodus 20:7, 2 Kings 18:13 - 19:37

Teaching Point: God's name describes his character and is not to be used carelessly.

WARM UP 1

Explain that you are allocating people to groups without using their names or pointing to them. Select two leaders and two children to do the choosing. They take it in turns to choose a person to join their group, by describing them without using their name. No derogatory descriptions allowed. When the person being described recognises their description they stand behind the group leader. Allow five minutes for the exercise to see who collects the largest group. Point out to the children how difficult it was to do this exercise without using names. Names are important and tell us who the person is. Ask the children how they feel if people use their name to poke fun at them.

Say, 'Today's true story from the Bible is about the most important name in the world. I want you to listen carefully so that you can tell me:

1. How did people use God's name carelessly (wrongly) in the story?
2. How do people use God's name carelessly today?'

CONSOLIDATION 1

The object of the game is for the children to act positively when a name is used carefully and do nothing if a name is used incorrectly.

Choose four people and place each one in a corner of the room. The children sit in the centre. One of the four calls out his/her name and all the children run to that person. The leader signals a different one of the four, who calls out his/her own name. The children run to the second person. Repeat randomly, getting faster and faster. Once the children understand the game, tell them that the people may call out their own name, or the name of another leader. If the person calls out his/her own name the children are to run to him/her as the person will have used his/her name correctly. If the person uses another leader's name the children stay where they are, as the name will have been used incorrectly. If the game is to be used to determine a winner, the last person to arrive at the person is out, as is anyone who moves when the name is used incorrectly.

WIND UP 1

Remind the children of the Warm Up and how difficult it was to choose people without using their names. Ensure that they understand the importance of names and what they tell us about the person. Review the questions from the Warm Up. Comment on the use of 'Oh, God' and 'Jesus' as swear words. (These are used frequently in the playground and on television.) Link in to the game and the consequences of using names incorrectly. Review the first three commandments.

ABOUT THE USE OF GOD'S NAME

Text: Read and study Exodus 20:7, 2 Kings 18:13 - 19:37

Teaching Point: God's name describes his character and is not to be used carelessly.

WARM UP 2

Show pictures of the Mr Men people, e.g. Mr Happy etc. Ask the children to identify them and tell you about them. Explain that, just as the Mr Men names tell us what they are like, so God's name tells us about his character. Instead of Mr Men books you can draw faces showing different emotions and label them Mr Happy, Miss Grumpy, etc. Discuss why it is important to use names correctly and not to poke fun at people. Say, 'Today's true story from the Bible is about the most important name in the world. Listen carefully so that you can tell me:

1. How did people use God's name carelessly (wrongly) in the story?
2. What were they saying about God's character?'

CONSOLIDATION 2

The object of the game is for the children to recognise one item as being special. Divide the children into teams and line them up at one end of the room. At the other end place a collection of miscellaneous items, e.g. table tennis balls, empty drinks bottles. There must be at least one item per team member and the same number of each item as there are teams, plus the one special item. As each item is called out, one member from each team runs to the end of the room to collect that item and bring it back to base. Finish when the only item remaining at the other end is the special item. This game can also be played by providing each team with a pillowcase containing a number of different small items. When the item is called out the team member has to locate it by feel. Each pillowcase must contain identical objects.

WIND UP 2

Remind the children of the Warm Up and how names can indicate character, e.g. Duncan means 'bearded warrior', Charles - the strong man, David - beloved, Richard - wealthy, powerful one, Margaret - a pearl, Emily - hard-working, Ruth - compassionate and beautiful. (Books on the meaning of names are available at libraries. It would be good to use the names of children in the group as examples.) Ensure that they understand the importance of God's name and what it tells us about him. Review the questions from the Warm Up. Comment on the use of 'Oh, God' and 'Jesus' as swear words. (These are used frequently in the playground and on television.) Link into the game and the importance of only collecting what was named, (or, if using the alternative game, the importance of responding appropriately to names). Review the first three commandments.

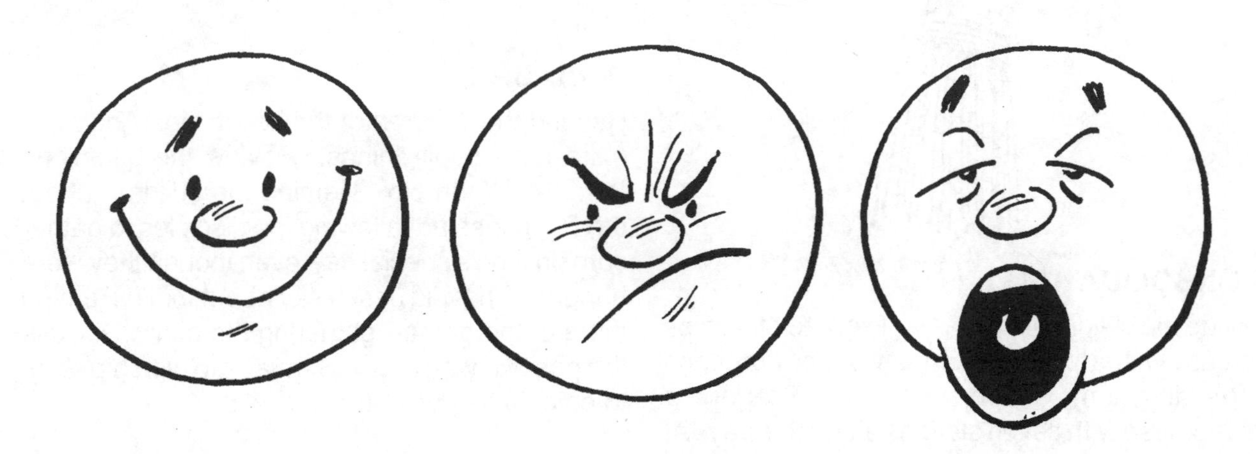

ABOUT THE USE OF GOD'S DAY

Text: Read and study Exodus 20:8-11, Luke 6:1-5; 14:1-6.

Teaching Point: God's day is special.

WARM UP 1

The object is to demonstrate legalism. Two leaders or older children are having a good time playing a common game, e.g. hopscotch or skipping. Another leader stops them and tells them they are not obeying all the rules and adds in a restriction. Repeat this several times. Each time the players try and keep the new rules. They repeat them to each other so that they do not forget them. In the end all they can do is stop the game and try and remember the rules. The game is no fun anymore.

In today's true story from the Bible we will see what happened when some people added in lots of extra rules.

1. Who were the people who added extra rules?
2. What rules did they add?
3. What did Jesus do about it?

CONSOLIDATION 1

Divide the children into teams. Prepare thin strips of card with a picture of an ear of corn on each (see diagram), seven per child. Prepare a racecourse with seven stations along the way. At each station deposit the same number of corn cards as there are children in the team. On the command, 'Harvest!' the first child in each team runs along the course, picking up the seven ears of corn as he goes. When he reaches the end the next child in line races along the course. The winning team is the first one to get all their team members through the harvest field having harvested their corn as they went.

WIND UP 1

Remind the children of the Warm Up. Adding in extra rules spoilt things. Review the questions from the Warm Up. Remind the children about the Pharisees not allowing the disciples to gather corn on God's special day, even though they were hungry. What did Jesus say about that? Remind them of the game - gathering the corn. Discuss the positive way to use Sunday - to worship God, to enjoy ourselves, to relax.

ABOUT THE USE OF GOD'S DAY

Text: Read and study Exodus 20:8-11, Luke 6:1-5; 14:1-16.

Teaching Point: God's day is special.

WARM UP 2

Introduce special clothes, special objects, special days. Discuss what is special about each thing. Show the children some objects that are symbolic of special days and celebrations. These can include candles, cake, party hats, presents, eggs, cross, carol music, Santa Claus hats, daffodils, male silhouette, big clock for midnight, red heart, chocolates, rings, rice, confetti, veil, mortar board, hat, gown, bread and wine. Ask the children to name special celebrations in the calendar year. Focus on one day which gets celebrated 52 or 53 times per year.

Say, 'In today's true story from the Bible, we will learn about a special day. When you come back, tell me what was special about the day and who said that it was a special day.'

CONSOLIDATION 2

Mark out an area and designate it as the rest area. Divide the children into small groups. Assign six different tasks and number them 1-6, e.g. Day 1 - move the table from A to B, Day2 - stack the chairs, Day 3 - dig the garden, Day 4 - pack your bags for school, Day 5 - swim like a fish, Day 6 - feed the animals. The actions can involve moving physical objects, miming, or a combination of both. When the leader shouts out a day number, the children perform the associated action. When Day 7 is called, the children stop work and go to the rest area where they sit down and recite, 'Keep Sunday special' seven times before returning to work. Find some way of rewarding the children and leaders at the end of the task.

WIND UP 2

Remind the children of the Warm Up, special things for special days. Review the questions from the Warm Up. Remind the children about the Pharisees not allowing the disciples to gather corn on God's special day, even though they were hungry. What did Jesus say about that? Remind them of the game. Discuss the positive way to use Sunday - to worship God, to enjoy ourselves, to relax.

ABOUT PARENTS

Text Exodus 20:12, 1Samuel 2:12-17,22-36; 4:1-11

Teaching Point To introduce the meaning of 'respect' and to show how seriously God views this commandment.

WARM UP 1

The object is to review the previous commandments and introduce the meaning of respect.

Prepare a large box containing a copy of one craft activity for each of the previous four commandments. You require also the first five commandments written on strips of card, one commandment per strip. Prior to the lesson prepare a pin board with 'God's Instructions' on a strip of card along the top, and 'respect' on a piece of card to the left. Pin up a tick at one side of 'respect' and a cross at the other. Prepare a series of six strips of card, each one containing one of the following: 'ignore', 'make fun of', 'try to trick', 'obey', 'try to please', 'listen to'. Remind the children that they have been learning about God's instructions to his people.

Review the reason for God's instructions (or rules) - to enable his people to live happily with him and with each other. Take the craft activities out of the treasure chest one at a time in the order of the commandments. Ask the children what each one is about, reviewing the Bible story and commandment it illustrates. At the end of each review one of the leaders pins up the appropriate commandment on the pin board. Once you have completed the review of the first four commandments, point out that they are to do with our relationship with God. The remaining six deal with our relationship with each other. See if anyone knows which commandment comes next. Pin up 'Respect your parents' under the other four on the pin board. Explain to the children that we are going to look at the meaning of respect. Read out the six cards one at a time, each time asking, 'Is this the way we show we respect someone?' Then pin the card under the tick or the cross.

When the exercise is completed tell the children that in today's true story from the Bible we will see what happens when two sons do not respect their father. Ask them to listen carefully so that they can answer the following questions:

1. What were the names of the two sons?
2. What was the father's name?
3. How did the sons break this commandment? *(they did not listen to Eli)*
4. What happened as a result? *(God punished them all)*

CONSOLIDATION 1

The children stand up. Using the six cards that teach the meaning of 'respect', call out the phrases one at a time in random order. If the phrase indicates respect the children remain standing, if disrespect, the children fall down flat. Continue for as long as required. Rather than standing or falling down you could designate two areas, marking one with a tick and the other with a cross. The children start in the middle and run to the appropriate symbol when the phrase is called out. Return to the middle after each phrase. Children making the wrong choice can be out for one turn.

WIND UP 1

Review the questions from the Warm Up. Refer back to the game to ensure that the children understand the meaning of respect. Rehearse the fifth commandment.

ABOUT PARENTS

Text Exodus 20:12, 1Samuel 2:12-17,22-36; 4:1-11

Teaching Point To show how seriously God views this commandment.

WARM UP 2

Show the children a picture of a head of state. Who is this? Who is he/she in charge of? Who does he/she have authority over? Show a picture of a lot of people. Does this mean that we have to obey him/her?

Show a picture of a schoolteacher. Who is this? Who does he/she have authority over? Show a picture of a lot of school children. Does this mean that we have to obey him/her?

Show a picture of a mum and dad. Who are they? Who do they have authority over? Show a picture of a couple of children. Does this mean that we have to obey them? Who has authority over the head of state? God. Remind the children that rules were given for our benefit. God knows how we should behave. God says we should obey our parents.

Say, 'In today's true story from the Bible we will see what happened when two people did not obey their father. I want you to come back and tell me:

1. What were the names of the two sons?
2. What was the father's name?
3. How did the sons break this commandment? *(they did not listen to Eli)*
4. What happened as a result? *(God punished them all)'*

CONSOLIDATION 2

The leader announces he/she is the dad/mum and they are all his/her children. A second leader is introduced as a non-parent. The children move around to music. When the music stops one of the two leaders calls out a command, e.g. 'stand on one leg', 'lie down', 'jump like a frog', etc.. If the 'parent' calls out the command the children must obey, if the non-parent calls out the command the children do nothing.

WIND UP 2

Review the questions from the Warm Up. God has said that we are to obey our parents. Refer back to the game. Obeying the leader was like respecting our parents by obeying them. Point out that God has given us rules for our benefit. Rehearse the fifth commandment.

ABOUT LIFE

Text: Read and study Exodus 20:13, Genesis 4: 1-16.

Teaching Point: Human life is a gift from God and is not ours to take away.

WARM UP 1

Two leaders act out the following scenario. Two children are playing with toys. One child snatches a toy that the other child is playing with. They fight over the toy. The child who snatched it loses out. This child has a minor tantrum and hits out at the other child, calling out, 'I hate you!' The main leader steps in and separates them.

Talk to the children about the wrongness of the behaviour. Say, 'In today's true story from the Bible we will find out what happened when someone was angry with his brother. I want you to come back and tell me:

1. What were the brothers' names?
2. Which commandment was broken?
3. What did God do about it?'

CONSOLIDATION 1

Start by reviewing the questions from the Warm Up. Point out that Jesus said that being really angry with someone was as bad as murdering them. Point out the need to say sorry when we have been really angry with someone. Play a team game. Set up an obstacle course with a leader standing in the way at some point. The only way to get past the leader and get to the end of course is to use a password. The password is 'sorry' and the leader answers, 'forgiven'.

WIND UP 1

Review the questions from the Warm Up. Remind the children of Jesus' comments about anger being as bad as murder. Refer back to the Warm Up as an example. Link in to the game and the need to say sorry. Discuss why saying sorry can be such a difficult thing to do. Rehearse the sixth commandment.

WARM UP 2

The object is to demonstrate the importance of following the maker's instructions. Produce a box containing some piece of electrical equipment or similar along with its instructions. You could use a Lego model with instructions instead. Decide that you do not need the instructions; you can make it work. Try and put piece of equipment or model together and get it all wrong. Eventually, go back to the instructions and get it right. Why did you get it wrong? You did not follow the maker's instructions. God is our maker; has given us instructions. Talk about the importance of following them. Revise the first five commandments.

Say, 'In today's true story from the Bible we will see what happened when someone broke one of God's instructions. I want you to come back and tell me:

1. Which commandment was broken?
2. Who broke the commandment?
3. What happened to him as a result?'

CONSOLIDATION 2

The object is to revise the order of the commandments. Pin up numbers 1 to 6 around the room. The children start in the centre. Call out a commandment and the children run to the correct number. Anyone running to the wrong place goes to the 'Sin Bin' and misses a turn.

WIND UP 2

Review the questions from the Warm Up. Remind the children of the importance of following the maker's instructions. Link in to the game. Rehearse the first six commandments.

ABOUT PURITY

Text: Read and study Exodus 20:14, 2 Sam 11:1 - 12:23.

Teaching Point: Taking someone else's husband or wife is wrong.

WARM UP 1

Have a huge biscuit tin and a single biscuit on display. Tell the children that the biscuits belong to two people - a rich man and a poor man. The biscuit tin belongs to the rich man and the single biscuit belongs to the poor man. A leader runs in with an urgent message to say that a friend is coming to tea. The rich man is overjoyed and sets a table, but uses the poor man's biscuit to put on the table next to the cup and saucer.

Say, 'In today's true story from the Bible we will find out about someone who did what the rich man did, took something precious belonging to someone else, when he had plenty of his own already. I want you to come back and tell me:

1. What was the name of the man?
2. What did he take?
3. What commandment was broken?'

CONSOLIDATION 1

Divide the children into pairs with one singleton. Leaders may need to partner smaller children. The singleton is blindfolded and has to tag one of the pairs. The person he touches is joined into a pair with the singleton and the other partner is blindfolded in his place. If children are unwilling, a leader may have to volunteer to be the singleton.

WIND UP 1

Review the questions from the Warm Up. Remind the children of the game. It was not nice to have your partner taken. Point out that sin makes marriage hard. (It is important to be sensitive to children from single parent families.) Rehearse the seventh commandment.

Lesson 32

ABOUT PURITY

Text: Read and study Exodus 20:14, 2 Sam 11:1 - 12:23.

Teaching Point: Adultery is wrong.

WARM UP 2

Ask the children to identify every person in the room who is wearing a ring. Bring these people to the front of the room and ask them how they acquired their rings. Concentrate on the wedding rings. Then lead into a discussion by asking the following questions:

Who has been to a wedding? Who has been a bridesmaid or pageboy? Who are the most important people at a wedding? What do they say? What do they do? *(Make promises to each other.)* What do they promise? What happens if they later break their promises? *(Divorce, separation, sadness.)*

Say, 'The word for breaking the promises you make when you get married is 'adultery'. God said, 'Do not commit adultery.' In today's true story from the Bible we will see what happened when someone broke that commandment. I want you to come back and tell me:

1. What was the name of the man?
2. What was the name of the woman?
3. What was the result of breaking the commandment?'

CONSOLIDATION 2

Ask the children to get into pairs and give each pair a large sheet of newspaper. They will probably pick someone of their own sex, but at this age that is the most natural example of a one to one relationship. The object is to stand on the flat sheet of paper and not fall off or touch the ground. Any pair touching the ground will be out. Repeat, but first fold the paper in half. Keep repeating until it becomes totally impossible. To stay on the longest, the pair will have to help each other. Finish by explaining that a marriage relationship should be like that, with each one helping the other so that they can both stay together, even when things are difficult.

WIND UP 2

Review the questions from the Warm Up. Remind the children of the game and the importance of working together if they were to survive. Point out that sin makes marriage hard. (It is important to be sensitive to children from single parent families.) Rehearse the seventh commandment.

ABOUT PROPERTY

Text: Read and study Exodus 20:15, Joshua 7:1-26.

Memory Verse: God said, 'Do not steal.' Exodus 20:15

Teaching Point: To teach that stealing is wrong.

WARM UP 1

To introduce the concept that behaviour has consequences. Prepare a large box containing craft activities for commandments 2-6 and two T-shirts. You also need the first seven commandments written on strips of card, one commandment per strip. Prior to the lesson prepare a pin board with 'God's Instructions' on a strip of card along the top. Start with an obedience game, e.g. 'Simon Says'. Whenever children get the instruction wrong they are out. Discuss the fact that disobeying instructions has consequences. Remind the children that they have been learning about God's instructions to his people. Review the reason for God's instructions - to enable his people to live happily with him and each other. Take the T-shirts from the box and ask the children to choose one for you to wear. Remind them about Joshua asking the people to choose something. What was it? Which commandment did we learn in that story? Pin up the first commandment. Take the craft activities out of the box one at a time in random order. Ask them what each one is about, reviewing the Bible story and commandment it illustrated. At the end of each review one of the leaders pins up the appropriate commandment. Once you have pinned up the seven commandments, ask the children to help you place them in the right order.

When the exercise is completed tell the children that in today's true story from the Bible we will learn about the next commandment God gave to his people. Ask them to listen carefully so that they can answer the following questions:

1. Which commandment was broken?
2. What was the name of the man who broke that commandment?
3. What happened as a result - to the man and his family and to God's people?

CONSOLIDATION 1

The aim of this team game is to review the story details and revise the memory verse. Prior to the lesson, divide the children into small groups, each group with one leader. Write one of the following words or figures onto a piece of paper, then photocopy them onto different coloured paper, one set for each small group: God said, 'Do not steal.' Exodus 20 15

Place the words in multicoloured sets of the same word or figure. Determine eight sites in the room for the children to run between. Prepare eight questions to elicit the main details of the story and after each question state which site the group is to go to in order to collect their colour word. If possible, each group should visit the sites in a different order.

Divide the children into their groups and give each leader a set of questions. After each question is answered the group runs to the designated site and collects their colour paper. The winner is the first team to collect all their pieces of paper and put them in the order of the memory verse.

WIND UP 1

Review the answers to the questions. Rehearse the memory verse.

ABOUT PROPERTY

Text: Read and study Exodus 20:15, Joshua 7:1-26.

Teaching Point: To teach that stealing is wrong.

WARM UP 2

Talk to the children about the series they are doing - God's Instructions. Review the reason why God gave rules - for our benefit. The first four are to do with our relationship with God, the remaining six with our relationship with other people. While all this is going on, a leader dressed as a burglar (mask, jeans and stripy jumper with a sack to put items in) flits through the area picking up coats, handbags, etc. that have been planted prior to the session and putting them in the sack. When the children call out to the leader that a burglar is there, the leader looking up in the wrong direction, asking, 'Where?' The leader disbelieves the children until eventually he spots the burglar, flitting off. The leader asks the children to check what is missing. Tell them not to worry, you'll get it sorted and get all the stuff back.

Say, 'In today's true story from the Bible we will find out what happened when someone took something that did not belong to them. I want you to listen carefully so that you can tell me:

1. What was the name of the man who stole what did not belong to him?
2. What did he steal?
3. What happened as a result - to the man and his family and to God's people?'

CONSOLIDATION 2

Remind the children that we must not take other people's property. Divide the children into groups and give each group a colour. Hide different coloured items around the room. The children have to find their colour items. Anyone taking someone else's coloured item is out of the game. The first group to collect all its items wins. You might want to prime some leaders to put the wrong coloured items in their team's pile to bring out the problem caused by stealing. When the wrong coloured items are discovered the leader who 'stole' them has to return them.

If time allows for a second run, ask the groups hide their articles, then give each group a different colour to collect.

WIND UP 2

Remind the children that God says that we should not take another person's property. Discuss the kind of property the children would be likely to want to take, such as sweets, rubbers, pens, etc. Review the questions from the Warm Up. Link in to the game and what happened if someone took the wrong coloured item. Rehearse the eighth commandment.

ABOUT TELLING LIES

Text: Read and study Exodus 20:16, 2 Kings 5:15-27.

Teaching Point: To teach the importance of always telling the truth.

WARM UP 1

Place the children into groups and call out a series of letters or numbers. The groups form the letter or number using their bodies. End with the number 9. Say, 'Today's true story from the Bible is about the 9th rule God gave to his people. I want you to listen carefully so that you can tell me:

1. What was the rule?
2. Who broke it?
3. What happened as a result?'

CONSOLIDATION 1

Prepare a collection of items such as table tennis balls, cards, pieces of paper, etc. There must be the same number of each item. Divide the children into teams plus a team of leaders and give each team the same number of items. When the leader calls out a number, one member of each team runs and puts that number of items into a bucket. Prime the leaders to cheat by occasionally depositing more than the number called. It does not matter if the children notice. Periodically stop and ask the players to tell you how many items they have deposited in the bucket. The leader lies about the number of items deposited. At the end of the game the leaders have run out of items. Point out that everyone started with the same number of items. The leaders have obviously deposited more than they should and lied about it. Give a reward to all the children, but the leaders miss out because they lied.

WIND UP 1

Review the questions from the Warm Up. Link in to the game. Point out how the leaders lied about breaking the rules when questioned and how it spoiled the game for everyone else.

ABOUT TELLING LIES

Text: Read and study Exodus 20:16, 2 Kings 5:15-27.

Teaching Point: To teach the importance of always telling the truth.

WARM UP 2

To illustrate why it is important to tell the truth. Prepare a treasure chest with six or seven objects that are easily identified by children, e.g. a boot, a football, a soft toy. Include an empty 2 Litre soft drink bottle. Bring out the items one at a time, identifying them as you do so. Identify the first item correctly, then identify some items correctly and others incorrectly, e.g. bring out the boot and say it is your slipper. Each time ask the children if you have told them the truth. Bring out the soft drink bottle last and tell the children it is a baseball or rounders bat, demonstrating how you would use it. When they tell you it is a soft drink bottle, tell them it is a different type of soft drink than is stated on the label. When they tell you that you are lying, say that it was only a little lie. Do little lies matter?

Once you have established that all lies matter, 'little' as well as 'big', ask the children why it matters if you do not always tell them the truth. Bring out that if they cannot trust you to tell them the truth, they will not know whether to believe you when you tell them about anything and, most importantly, about God.

In today's true story from the Bible we will learn what happened to a man who lied. Send them off to Bible time with the following questions:

1. What was the name of the man who lied?
2. Who did he lie to? *(Naaman and Elisha)*
3. What happened to him as a result?

CONSOLIDATION 2

A team game to revise the order of the first nine commandments. Divide the children into groups of nine. Prepare one set of commandments for each group, writing the commandments on separate pieces of paper. If possible, use different coloured paper for each team. Prepare an obstacle course for each team (see diagram).

The team starts at Elisha's house, climbs over the hill (a chair or large cushion), wriggles through the valley (under a table) and takes the stepping stones (carpet squares or similar) to Naaman (a leader). Naaman gives the child one of the commandments and the child returns to Elisha's house along the same route. When the child reaches Elisha's house the next child sets off for Naaman. The winning team is the first one to collect all nine commandments and place them in the correct order.

WIND UP 2

Remind the children of the Warm Up and why it matters if you lie. Review the questions from the Warm Up. Remind them of the game. Rehearse the first nine commandments.

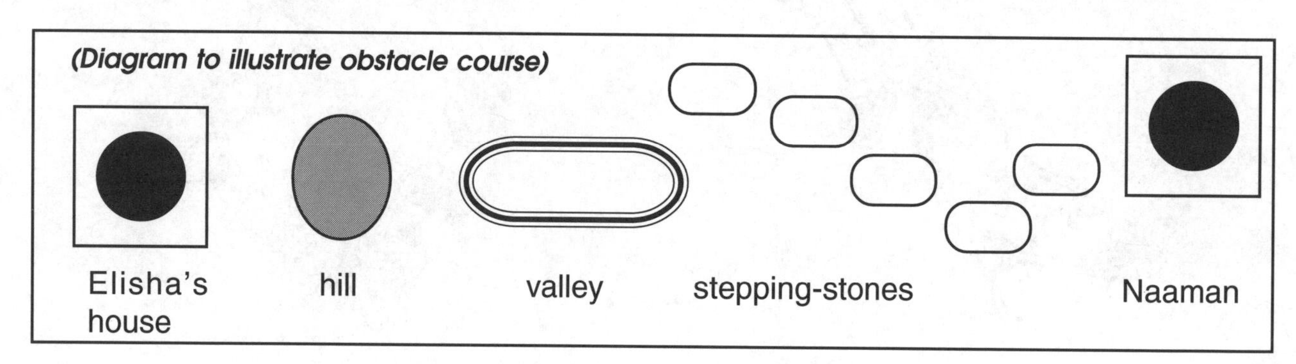

ABOUT BEING CONTENT

Text: Read and study Exodus 20:17, 1Kings 21:1-19.

Teaching Point: We must not want others' things so badly that we can think of nothing else.

WARM UP 1

One of the leaders dresses up as a golfer, complete with plastic golf clubs and table tennis balls for golf balls. Place a proper set of golf clubs in a golf bag to one side. Explain that the purpose of golf is to hit a ball from the tee to the hole on the green, using as few strokes as possible. If the ball looks as though it will hit someone, the golfer calls out 'Fore' as a warning. Ask the children to cover their heads with their arms every time you call out, 'Fore'. Do it a few times for practice. Then softly hit a few balls over the heads of the children, calling out, 'Fore' each time. Explain that the reason you are hitting the children with the balls is because you have bad clubs. If only you had clubs like the ones at the side, you would be able to play much better. Spend a little time coveting the good clubs, before sending the children off to Bible time.

Say, 'In today's true story from the Bible we will see what happened when someone really wanted something that did not belong to him. I want you to listen carefully so that you can tell me:

1. What was the name of the man?
2. What did he want?
3. How did he get it?
4. What did God say about it?'

CONSOLIDATION 1

Game 1 Place a collection of uninteresting items in the centre of the room, along with some wrapped sweets or other desirable items. Form the children into a ring around the outside of the room and number them off 1-4 in turn around the circle. Show the children the sweets. Talk about how delicious they are and tell them that they belong to you. No one else is to have one. If anyone takes a sweet they are out. Tell the children that the object of the game is to collect all the items apart from the sweets. As each number is called the child with that number runs into the centre and collects the same number of items, e.g. number 2 collects two items, number 4 collects four items, etc. Any child who collects one of the desirable items is out.

Game 2 Sit the children in a ring. Show the children the sweets as above. Give each child a sweet and reinforce the fact that the sweets do not belong to them and they are not to eat them. The children pass a box from hand to hand around the circle to music. When the music stops the child holding the box puts his sweet into the box.

WIND UP 1

Review the questions from the Warm Up. Ask the children if they can remember what you called out when you hit the balls over their heads. Point out that there were four commandments broken in the Bible story. Go over the four commandments *(Do not murder, do not steal, do not lie, do not covet)*. Rehearse all 10 commandments. Hand out the sweets from the Consolidation.

ABOUT BEING CONTENT

Text: Read and study Exodus 20:17, 1Kings 21:1-19.

Teaching Point: To introduce story details and revise the 10 commandments.

WARM UP 2

Prior to the lesson place nine vegetables and a bunch of grapes in a box (or treasure chest). The items can be real, squeaky toys or pictures. Bring them out one at a time, asking the children to identify them, and place them on a table. Ask the children which one is different. Say, 'Today's true story from the Bible is about grapes and vegetables. I want you to come back and tell me:

1. What do grapes and vegetables have to do with the Bible story?
2. What was the name of the king?
3. Which commandments were broken?'

CONSOLIDATION 2

The object of the game is to find the 10 commandments and put them in order. Divide the children into teams and provide one set of commandments for each team, each set on a different colour paper. Hide the commandments under a large sheet or parachute in the centre of the room. The team members take it in turns to run into the centre, wriggle under the parachute and collect one of their colour commandments. Any wrong colour that is collected has to be returned by the next player. The first team to collect their set of commandments and put them in the correct order wins.

WIND UP 2

Review the questions from the Warm Up. Remind the children that the purpose of God's rules is to maximise our relationship with God and with one other, not to be a burden (1 John 5:3). Rehearse all 10 commandments.

THE RESULT OF UNBELIEF

Text: Read and study Numbers 13:1 - 14:10; 14:26-38.

Teaching Point: God punishes unbelief.

WARM UP 1

The leader challenges the children to beat him at the game. Place 13 pieces of fruit (either real or play) on a table. The contestants can take any number from one to three pieces at any one go, but the person to take the last piece loses. The child has to start first. Whatever the child takes, the leader takes enough to make a total of four fruit picked up at that go. Then the child is bound to be left with the last one. Do this with several different volunteers.

Talk about being discouraged when you just cannot win. Say, 'In today's true story from the Bible God's people felt just like that. They just knew they could not win. I want you to listen carefully and come back and tell me:

1. What did God want his people to do?
2. Why did he want them to do something they felt they couldn't do?
3. What did they forget about God?'

CONSOLIDATION 1

Divide the children into multi-age teams and give them instructions to search out the land. Hidden around the room will be 12 strips of card that make up Numbers 14:11 (GNB). You need one set for each group. Each strip of card has a picture of a piece of fruit on the other side. Split the verse up as follows:

HOW LONG WILL / THESE PEOPLE / TREAT ME / WITH CONTEMPT? / HOW LONG / WILL THEY REFUSE / TO BELIEVE IN ME, / IN SPITE OF ALL / THE MIRACULOUS SIGNS /I HAVE PERFORMED / AMONG THEM? / NUMBERS 14:11

The fruit is placed on the cards in the following order - apple, banana, cherries, grapes, lemon, melon, oranges, pear, pineapple, plum, raspberry, strawberry.

The younger children are sent out to collect the 12 different fruit and the older children put the fruit in alphabetical order. Turn over to discover the Bible verse. The first team to complete the exercise wins.

WIND UP 1

Review the Warm Up, reminding the children how discouraging it was to always lose. Review the questions from the Warm Up. Remind the children about the spies collecting fruit from the land to show what a good land it was. Link in to the game. Discuss God's reaction to his people's lack of belief (Numbers 14:11).

THE RESULT OF UNBELIEF

Text: Read and study Numbers 13:1 - 14:10; 14:26-38.

Teaching Point: Those who refuse to put their trust in God miss out on the blessings.

WARM UP 2

Two leaders act out a situation demonstrating the relationship between God and the Israelites. Leader 1 talks about their friendship - remember the good things I've done for you, have I ever let you down? Leader 2 itemises the way Leader 1 has helped, e.g. hungry - gave me a burger, thirsty - gave me a drink, protection - stopped people bullying, kept promise - took to the zoo, showed the way when got lost, etc. With each incident Leader 1 reinforces what happened - yes, I did that, have I ever let you down? At the end Leader 2 admits Leader 1 has never let him down. Leader 1 checks Leader 2 is sure of this. Leader 1 tells Leader 2, 'I want you to go over there and open that tin. It contains good things that I want to give you.' Leader 2 dithers - not sure, perhaps it will contain things I don't like. Leader 1 - have I ever let you down? Leader 2 - no, but ...Eventually Leader 2 refuses to look in the tin and walks out. Leader 1 calls Leader 2 back and opens the tin, which is full of sweets. Leader 2 loves sweets, but it is too late - he has missed out.

In today's true story from the Bible we will see what happened when God's people did not do what God said. Send the children off to class with the following questions:

1. What did God want to give his people?
2. Why did they not do what God said?
3. What was the result?
4. (For older children) Why should they have trusted God?

CONSOLIDATION 2

Obedience leads to a reward; disobedience means missing out. Everyone who takes part will be rewarded. Prepare an obstacle course around the room and send the children through it one at a time at 5-10 second intervals. At the end of the course the children pick up a reward. Those who do not wish to take part miss out on the reward.

WIND UP 2

Review the questions from the Warm Up prior to the game. After the game remind the children of the Warm Up - Leader 2 missed out on the sweets because he did not trust Leader 1 and do what he said. Talk about the game - everyone who took part (obeyed the rules) obtained the blessing (a sweet).

GOD FORGIVES SIN

Text: Read and study Numbers 21:4-9, John 3:14-16.

Teaching Point: There is only one way to obtain forgiveness of sin.

WARM UP 1

Puppets or skit on wrongdoing having consequences (see script on page 92). Toby is looking for Trudy. Eventually she appears. Toby looks down at her feet (behind the screen) and sees that she has something attached to her foot. She has caught her foot in a trap. Trudy asks him to help her take it off. Toby wants to know why she is caught in the trap. After a lot of hemming and hawing, Trudy explains that she was just going to taste the grapes in the greenhouse when... Toby breaks in to remind her that Dad had told them to stay away from the greenhouse. Trudy says that the grapes looked so delicious that she had to try one. She was in the process of doing this when she heard Dad coming. In her haste to escape she caught her foot in the trap. Toby says that the only way out of the trap is to find Dad and ask him to take it off. He goes off with Trudy.

Say, 'In today's true story from the Bible we will learn about some people who turned against God and did not trust him to look after them. I want you to come back and tell me:

1. What did they do wrong?
2. What were the consequences of their wrongdoing?
3. How could they obtain forgiveness?'

CONSOLIDATION 1

Play pass the parcel. Prepare one parcel for every 20 children. Sit in a circle of not more than 20, or several circles if lots of children. Each circle needs to be supervised by a leader. Pass the parcel around the circle. When the music stops the child with the parcel unwraps one layer. Inside the layer is a strip of paper containing a wrong action, such as disobeying parents, lying, stealing, etc. Along with the action is a penalty, such as seven push-ups. Either the child performs the penalty, or he can ask a leader to perform the penalty for him. Continue until the parcel is completely unwrapped. In the centre of the parcel is a cross. There is no penalty, because Jesus has taken it for us.

WIND UP 1

Remind the children of the Warm Up and the consequences of Trudy's wrongdoing. Review the questions from the Warm Up. Discuss the game. How did the child feel when the leader took his punishment? Who has taken our punishment? Remind the children that Jesus' death on the cross is the only way that we can obtain forgiveness and be friends with God.

GOD FORGIVES SIN

Text: Read and study Numbers 21:4-9, John 3:14-16.

Teaching Point: There is only one way to obtain forgiveness of sin.

WARM UP 2

Leaders take it in turns to say why they are acceptable to God. If there are only a couple of leaders, do it turn and turn about. Each time put on a different hat, to show you are a different person. Suggested statements:

I've got lots of money, so I'm all right. God will accept me.

I pray three times a day, so I'm all right. God will accept me.

I go to church twice on Sunday, so I'm all right. God will accept me.

I'm a good person, so I'm all right. God will accept me.

I read the Bible everyday, so I'm all right. God will accept me.

I'm a very important person, so I'm all right. God will accept me.

After each statement, ask the children to say if they think it is right. In today's true story from the Bible we will find out the only way we can be acceptable to God.

CONSOLIDATION 2

Divide the children into teams. The teams have to cross the river, by being pulled along in a boat (a plastic sledge or a washing basket with a rope). After 30 seconds snakes (leaders) slither out to trap the boats. The only way past is the password, 'Jesus died for me.' When each child reaches the other side of the river they are only allowed into safety if they use the password. For small children the password could be 'Jesus', or 'Jesus died'. The leader whispers the password to each child before they embark in the boat.

Alternatively, divide the children into groups and see which group can make the longest snake by threading cardboard tubes onto string.

WIND UP 2

Remind the children of the Warm Up. Did any of the leaders get it right? What is the only way to obtain forgiveness of sin? Discuss the game. What was the password they needed to get to safety? Remind the children that Jesus' death on the cross is the only way that we can obtain forgiveness and be friends with God.

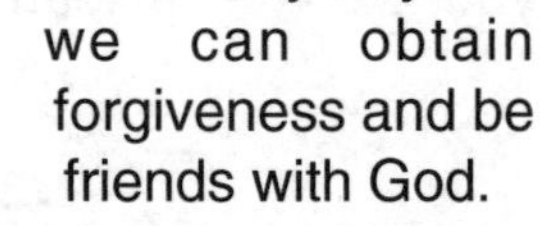

THE RESULT OF FAITH

Text: Read and study Joshua 1:1 - 2:24; 3:14-17.

Teaching point: God rewards faith in him.

WARM UP 1

In front of the children make up a jug of gunge (a viscous or liquid material), using such things as flour, engine oil, wood shavings, old nails, etc. Ask for volunteer(s) to help. Do the volunteers trust the leader not to empty the jug of gunge over them? Get a second leader to volunteer. Does the volunteer trust the leader not to empty the jug over him? Then reverse the situation. Does the leader trust the volunteer not to empty the jug over him? Do not reverse the situation with the children!

Say, 'Today's true story from the Bible is about someone who trusted God. I want you to come back and tell me:

1. How many men went to spy out the land?
2. What was the name of the woman?
3. How did the men escape?
4. How did the woman escape?'

CONSOLIDATION 1

Make three or four dens with tables turned on their sides or chairs in circles. Two leaders are soldiers. Depending on numbers, divide the children between two, three or four dens. On command, the children must rush from their den to an adjacent one. Captured children are sent to the 'Sin Bin' for 1-2 minutes and then released by the leader to rejoin the game.

WIND UP 1

Review the questions from the Warm Up. Comment that God provided a way of escape for the woman in a difficult situation. Her reward was to live when everyone else in her town died. She knew what God was going to do. She trusted God. Do the children trust God like Rahab did?

WARM UP 2

Tell the children that you've had a hard time at work; list some imaginary, easily understood tasks that you've accomplished. Ask them to guess what you would best like as a reward. Put up some pictures, such as lying on a beach, hotel (weekend away), special meal, box of chocolates, new racing bike, etc. Which one would the children like best? They must come back to find out your choice. Say, 'Today's true story from the Bible is about a woman who got a reward. Come back and tell me:

1. What was her name?
2. What was her reward?
3. What did she do to get her reward?'

CONSOLIDATION 2

Remind the children of the spies who entered Jericho via the gates and left via a window in the city wall. Set up a game area with a wide entrance (gates) bordered by chairs, etc. and a narrower exit (window) at the other end. The children are spies escaping from the soldiers. The leader is the chief soldier and stands at the other side of the window with his back turned to the children. Starting at the gates, the children slither on their tummies in a race for the window. When the leader says, 'I see SPIES', he turns around quickly on the word 'spies'. Any children seen moving must return to the beginning. Other leaders ensure compliance.

WIND UP 2

Reintroduce the pictures from the Warm Up. Ask children to guess your favourite reward. Tell them which you chose and why. Do they like rewards? Today's story was not about a luxury reward, but something far more important - life itself. Review the Warm Up questions.

THE RESULT OF OBEDIENCE

Text: Read and study Joshua 5:13 - 6:25.

Teaching Point: The importance of obeying God's word.

Lesson 39

WARM UP 1

Prepare signs with commands, such as 'stand', 'stack boxes', 'sit', 'hop', 'stretch', 'turn around', etc. Place these around the room and point to them, or hold them up as necessary. Initially, nothing is said; there is no introduction. Only the signs are used, which the children must obey. This should unnerve the children, because they will not be sure what to do. Eventually the leader says, 'It's important to obey God's commands, even if we don't **always** understand why.'

Say, 'Today's true story from the Bible is about something that God asked his people to do. Come back later and tell me:

1. What did the Israelites have to do to obey God?
2. Did they obey God?
3. What happened as a result?'

CONSOLIDATION 1

Open out a parachute or sheet and form a wall around it with boxes. Leave only the cords of the parachute or the edges of the sheet showing. Place sweets on the parachute inside the wall as a temptation (parallel with the silver, gold and bronze articles). Issue instructions on how to destroy the wall (see below). Tell the children to bring anything inside the wall to the leader - it's not for them!

Instructions on how to destroy the wall:

1. Bombard with cushions or similar. (Place the children a long way away.)
2. Knock down with bludgeons (cardboard tubes). (Place the children out of reach.)
3. Bombard with table tennis balls from fairly close.
4. March once around the wall then back to base.
5. March twice, three times, etc. around the wall then back to base.
6. March seven times around the wall.

On the seventh time, tell the children to give a big shout, then pull the cords or the sheet edge to topple the boxes. For an alternative Consolidation, walk seven times around the outside of the church. Clap hands and shout on the seventh time. Why doesn't it fall down? Because God didn't say it would!

WIND UP 1

Remind the children about the Warm Up. Concentrate on the fact that we do not always know how God is going to achieve his purposes, but we know that he will. Review the questions from the Warm Up. Link in to the game and how God caused the walls of Jericho to fall down. Distribute the 'treasure' that they brought to you from within the walls.

THE RESULT OF OBEDIENCE

Text: Read and study Joshua 5:13 - 6:25.

Teaching Point: The importance of obeying God's word.

WARM UP 2

Using an OHP, place 13 matches in a circle. Ask the children if they can guess what that circle represents. Ask them to count the number of matches.

Say, 'Today's true story from the Bible is about a circle and the number thirteen. I want you to come back and tell me:

1. What does the circle represent?
2. What does the number 13 have to do with the Bible story?'

If you do not have an OHP, show the children 6-8 small objects, such as plastic fruit, etc. Place a pot or small bucket over each. Move them about. Ask the children to guess what's under each pot. For correct guesses take out the item and place it on top of the pot. Continue until all items have been identified. After the first two items have been correctly guessed, deliberately misidentify the children's guesses, e.g. when they say an item is under bucket no. 5, look under bucket no. 4. At the end explain that they would have found it easier and less frustrating if you had done what they said.

Say, 'In today's true story from the Bible we will see if God's people did what he said. Come back and tell me:

1. What did God tell the Israelites to do?
2. Did they obey him?
3. What was the result?'

CONSOLIDATION 2

Divide the children into groups. Make up a set of signs with numbers 1 to 15 (excluding 7), two plus signs and two minus signs, one set per group. Place the cards face down on the floor. The first child from each team runs to their cards, picks one up and returns to base with the card. Then the second child does the same and so on. The team and their leader arrange the cards to add up to 7, e.g. 10-8+1+4. The first team to get to 7 wins.

WIND UP 2

Review the questions from the Warm Up. Ask them why they were making 7 in the game? Remind the children that Israel had to obey God, even though it must have seemed a strange way to win a battle. We must obey God, even though we may not always understand God's ways.

NOT ASKING GOD'S GUIDANCE

Text: Read and study Joshua 9:1-27.

Memory Verse: We will serve the Lord our God. We will obey his commands. Joshua 24:24

Teaching point: We need to ask God for wisdom and guidance.

Lesson 40

WARM UP 1

Someone comes in dressed as a person with a specific and obvious role, such as a farmer, a tramp, an admiral, a postman. During a brief conversation the leader asks the person about his role. It soon becomes obvious that the person is a fraud. After the person leaves, the leader asks the children if they believe the person. They do not. The leader argues strongly, but unconvincingly, that the person really is a farmer, tramp, etc. The question is left open.

Say, 'Today's true story from the Bible is about some people who said they were from a certain country. Come back and tell me:

1. Who were the people?
2. What evidence did they give to show that they were from that country?
3. What did the Israelites forget to do?'

CONSOLIDATION 1

Write the memory verse, one word per paper shape, onto shapes of wineskins, sandals, loaves of bread and clothes. *'We will serve the Lord our God. We will obey his commands. Joshua 24:24.'* You require one set for each group, colour coded for age groups and classes. Hide the pieces around the room, retaining one piece from each set. The children are directed to search for their coloured pieces and bring each piece when found to their class leader to make up their memory verse. After a while, when the children are unable to find the final piece, the leader stops the game and asks what's the problem. The leader produces the missing pieces. The children protest, but the leader tells them it was enjoyable seeing them unable to complete the verse! They could have asked you for help, but they didn't. (Commend any child that did.)

WIND UP 1

Pick up on whether the children believed the person in the Warm Up was genuine. Explain that you have since discovered he was a fraud. You were deceived. Review the questions from the Warm Up. Explain that we can be deceived if we do not have the full picture. The Israelites were deceived because they did not seek God's guidance, just as the children had not sought help from the leader in the game.

NOT ASKING GOD'S GUIDANCE

Text: Read and study Joshua 9:1-27.

Teaching point: We need to ask God for wisdom and guidance.

WARM UP 2

Lay out a course using string or rope markers (see diagram). Blindfold a leader and ask him to walk the course without stepping outside the lines. He fails. He tries again with verbal guidance from another leader and succeeds.

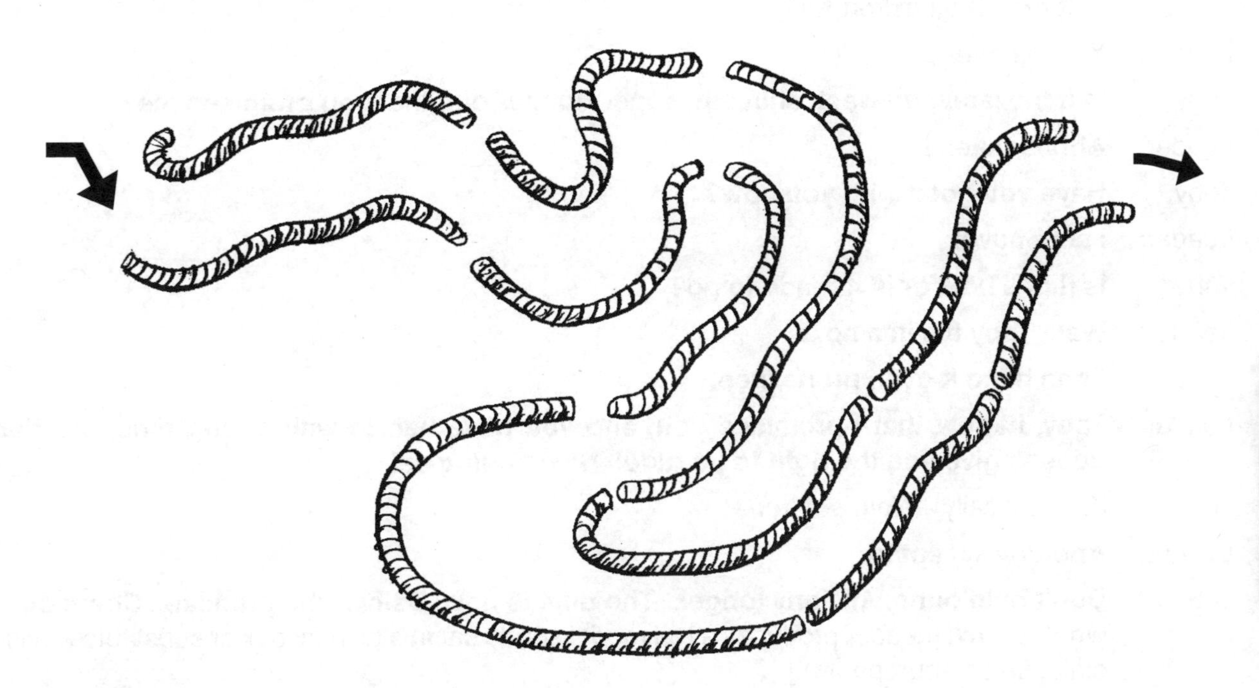

Say, 'In today's true story from the Bible we will see what happened when God's people took a decision without asking God for help. Come back and tell me:

1. What decision did the Israelites take?
2. What was the result?'

CONSOLIDATION 2

Divide the children into multi-age teams. Blindfold three or four volunteers, team by team, and ask them to go along the above course with verbal guidance from their teammates. The other teams sit on both sides of the lines and give false guidance to lead them astray. Each team has a go and, time permitting, the guides and those blindfolded then reverse roles.

WIND UP 2

Pick up on the game and how difficult it is to get things right without guidance, such as training in a sport, music, maths, history, etc. Review the questions from the Warm Up. Point out that we need to ask God to guide and help us to live in a way that is pleasing to him day by day.

Lesson 40

GOD PROVIDES

The leader is standing by a table, telling the children about a special toy car that he has found for his friend, Toby. He has been looking for it for a whole year. He is really excited because he has just found the very one he was looking for. He has sent a message to Toby to tell him about it. There is a loud knocking off stage.

Toby: [shouts offstage] **I am here!** [Toby enters.]

Leader: **Well hullo, Toby. Boys and girls, say hullo to Toby.**

Toby: **Hullo, boys and girls.** [Turns to leader.] **Have you got it? I have been waiting one whole year for this! Twelve long months, 365** tortuous **days, 8760 stagnant hours. I want it so much that I can taste it. Gimme, gimme, gimme.**

Leader: **Hold it, Toby. Hold it! I know you have been waiting a long, long time for it and now here it is.**

Toby: **Is it red, like I asked for?**

Leader: **Yes, all over.**

Toby: **Is it the latest, newest, shiniest, super dooper one that you promised me?**

Leader: **Abbbsolutely!**

Toby: **Have you got it with you now?**

Leader: **I sure have!**

Toby: **Is it in a box, or is it ready to go?**

Leader: **Well, Toby it's in a box.**

Toby: **Then hand it over, prune face!**

Leader: **Toby, I know that I promised you, and you have had to wait a long time, but that doesn't give you the right to be rude! Now apologise!**

Toby: [Sarcastically] **Well, sorrreee!**

Leader: **Apology accepted.**

Toby: **Don't hold out on me any longer. The time is now. Deliver the promise. Come on. I want it now!** [Leader produces a red model sports car in a display box or substitute (revise dialogue as appropriate).]

Leader: **Here it is. Do you like it?**

Toby: **It is fantastic. It's really great. Boy, is it cool! Cool! Cool!**

Leader: **Toby, I'm so pleased that you are happy and that you've got what you wanted. Especially as you've had to wait such a long time, and not so patiently. But, there is a small, teeny weeny problem.**

Toby: [Looking at the car.] **Nothing's going to matter now I've got the car. Getting the car was what I was worried about. What's the problem?**

Leader: **I need the car back.**

Toby: **What do you mean, you need the car back? How long for?**

Leader: **Permanently! Forever!**

Toby: **Nooooo! You can't do that. I've waited and waited and waited. I can't live without it. You ask too much. I cannot do it. You're unfair. I won't do it.**

Leader: **If you love me, you will trust me and do as I ask.**

JACOB TRUSTING GOD

Toby appears with a dismembered soft toy dangling down from one hand. He looks furtively left, right, up and down. Guilt is evident.

Toby: [whispers audibly] **Has anyone seen Trudy?** [Pauses]

Has anyone seen Trudy? Sssh. I borrowed her favourite soft toy while she was out. While I was playing steamrollers with it, its eyes fell out, its legs came off and its arm lengthened and .... Would you believe the stuffing came out? They don't make soft toys like they used to. Do you think she will be pleased with me? [Audience responds] **Do you think she will be angry with me?** [Audience responds] **I think you're right!** [Toby starts to quiver and shake uncontrollably.]

Trudy: [Offstage] **Toby!** [Distant call. Toby's quivering increases] **Toby!** [Louder call. Toby's quivering increases.] **Toby!!** [Shouting. Toby almost at fainting stage.]

Trudy comes into sight.

Toby: [hoarsely] **Here I am, Trudy.**

Trudy: **Boy, do you look frightened!**

Toby: **Would you like a chocolate bar?**

Trudy: **I smell a rat!**

Toby: [wheedling] **A big, sweet, calorie free bar.**

Trudy: **Why are you shaking so much and being so nice to me?**

Toby: **Full of caramel, nuts, raisins and smooth chocolate?**

Trudy: **OK, peanut brain, what are you up to?**

Toby: **I have just realised how wonderful a friend you are, and I would like to give you this token of my love.** [Aside] **Yuk!**

Trudy: **I think I should discuss this with Freud, my favourite soft toy. By the way, have you seen him?**

Toby: [Starts shaking violently and speaks very quietly] **No.**

Trudy: **What did you say?**

Toby: [Shaking and the words almost rung out of him, very loudly] **No!**

Trudy: [Looks down and sees the dangling rag] **Look, someone has left the washing out. It has the same colours in it as my special soft toy, Freud.**

Toby: [Shaking violently] **Two chocolate bars, a lollypop and my football kit.**

Trudy: **It is Freud.**

Toby: **A bicycle. I'll do all your homework for a year. My favourite computer game.**

Trudy: **What have you done to Freud?**

Toby: **My steamroller has genetically modified him.**

Trudy: [In a rage] **He is dead, kaput, and useless. My poor Freud!**

Toby: [Shaking uncontrollably] **CPR might work.**

Trudy: Did you do this?

The leader intervenes and draws the skit to an end.

JOSEPH GIVEN HIGH OFFICE

Toby: **Hello, boys and girls. Have you seen Trudy? I've got something important to tell her.** [calls] **Trudy! Where are you?** [pause] **Is she sitting at the back there? Bother! She's never there when you want her. Will you help me call her? On the count of 3 call, 'Trudy! Where are you?' One, two, three. Trudy! Where are you? That wasn't loud enough! Try again. One, two, three. Trudy! Where are you?**

Trudy enters.

Trudy: **Why are you calling/ What's the matter? Is the house on fire, or something?** [notices the children] **Oh, hello, boys and girls. Nice to see you again.**

Toby: **Trudy, listen to what I have to tell you. Something exciting happened to me today.**

Trudy: **Are you sure? You're always on about 'ever so exciting' things that you've done, Toby. And often I don't think they're all that exciting.**

Toby: **No, really, Trudy. I did such a brave thing today. I've been a hero.**

Trudy: **I bet you never were.**

Toby: **I was so. Just listen and I'll tell you all about it. I was on my way to football and ...**

Trudy: [interrupting] **Not another football story. It's all you ever talk about!**

Toby: **Listen, will you? I was on my way to football training and I had to go through the park.**

Trudy: **So?**

Toby: **I was going along, dribbling my football and minding my own business when ...**

Trudy: [in a bored tone] **What? I suppose something really exciting happened?**

Toby: **Well it did, actually. I heard a cry for help.**

Trudy: **Did you really? What was wrong?**

Toby: **I looked round, but couldn't see anyone. But I could hear this girl crying, 'Help! Help!' So I followed the cries, and what do you think I found?**

Trudy: **I don't know. What did you find?**

Toby: **A little girl with her back to a tree and a great big dog in front of her barking his head off.**

Trudy: **Toby, that's dreadful. What did you do?**

Toby: **I rescued her.**

Trudy: **Toby that was awfully brave of you.**

Toby: **Yes, wasn't it? She was ever so grateful. She called me her saviour.**

Trudy: **How did you rescue her? Did the dog bite you?**

Toby: **No. I told the dog to go away - and it did!**

Trudy: **Oh, Toby, you were brave. What sort of dog was it?**

Toby: **A really big, fierce one with a very loud bark.**

Trudy: **You've already said that. I mean what type was it? A Great Dane? An Alsatian?**

Toby: **Um, it was a little smaller than that.**

Trudy: **How much smaller?**

Toby: **Sort of terrier size. But it was fierce.**

Trudy: **So how did you get rid of this big, fierce dog?**

Toby: **I kicked my football down the path and the dog chased after it. It wanted to play. The little girl called me her hero.**

Trudy: **Well I think you really were a hero, Toby. Wasn't it a good thing that you were walking through the park at just that moment?**

Toby: **Yes, I definitely was in the right place at the right time.**

GOD DEMONSTRATES HIS POWER

Trudy: **Hi, boys and girls. Have you seen my brother, Toby? I've just got in from school. I had a lovely day. All my favourite lessons - maths, science, history. Ooh, I love school and homework. And my teacher, Mr Blenkinsop, is really clever and nice. I wonder where Toby is? He's always late home. He's hopeless. He's not good, like me. He's always being naughty. Do you know? Instead of doing his homework he plays football!**

Toby: [offstage] **Trudy, Trudy, where are you?**

Toby enters.

Trudy: **There you are! About time too.**

Toby: **Eh? What's wrong? I haven't done anything. Girls! You're all the same.**

Trudy: **Where have you been? You're late! I've been home for ages, haven't I boys and girls?**

Toby: **Never mind about that! I've had a great day. I scored a brilliant goal at lunchtime. I got the ball and I dribbled down the field. I passed Tim, then George, then Max** [insert leaders' or other children's names]. **Then I shot for goal. It flew into the corner of the net. It was fantastic, Trudy. Just like you see on the tele.**

Trudy: **Did you really?**

Toby: **Well, it might not have happened just like that - but I did score a goal!**

Trudy: **Well done. Oh, Toby! Mr Blenkinsop said to remind you that we've got a spelling test tomorrow?**

Toby: **You're joking! I'm going off to play football. We've got a match tomorrow after school. Bye!**

Toby exits.

Trudy: **But Toby ...**

Leader: **Same time the next day.**

Trudy: **Have you seen Toby anywhere, boys and girls? He's late again. Mr Blenkinsop wanted to see him after class this afternoon. I got 20 out of 20 in the spelling test.**

Toby enters, head hanging down.

Trudy: **Where have you been? It's awfully late.**

Toby: **You know Mr Blenkinsop wanted to see me?**

Trudy: **Yes.**

Toby: **It was about my spellings.**

Trudy: **What did you get?**

Toby: **I got two right.**

Trudy: **Toby, that's dreadful.**

Toby: **I know. I did so badly that Mr Blenkinsop made me stay behind after school and learn them.**

Trudy: **Well, I did tell you we had a test. You could have learnt your spellings last night if you'd only believed me.**

Toby: **It's not fair! I missed the football match.** [Exits looking unhappy.]

GOD DESTROYS HIS ENEMIES

The leader introduces two friends who have come to visit this morning, Toby and Trudy. *Trudy appears and looks round.*

Trudy: **Hello, boys and girls. Do you know, I got up really early this morning. I just couldn't sleep, 'cos I'm so excited.** [Looks round.] **Have you seen my brother, Toby?** [Calls] **Toby! Toby!**
Pause while nothing happens.

Trudy: **Perhaps if you all give him a call he'll come. All together now, Toby! Toby! That wasn't loud enough. Try again. On the count of 3 call out, Toby, where are you? 1, 2, 3, Toby, where are you?**
Enter Toby.

Toby: **What's all that noise for? Anybody would think I'm deaf!** [Looks around.] **Hello, Trudy. Who are all those boys and girls?**

Trudy: **It's the Sunday School, Toby. Don't you remember?** (Leader's name) **asked us if we'd like to come to Sunday School with her.**

Toby: **I'm too tired to remember.** [Yawns.] **It's still too early in the morning.**

Trudy: **You are hopeless, Toby. I've been up for hours. Ooh, I'm so excited.**

Toby: **What about?**

Trudy: **Surely you haven't forgotten, Toby? Aunt Mary is coming to take us to the zoo.**

Toby: **Since when?**

Trudy: **Since forever. Don't you remember? She wrote to Mum and Dad ages ago. She's going to take us to London Zoo, and she's coming today. That's why we had to call you. We've got to get ready.**

Toby: **I do remember Mum saying something about that. Are you sure it's today?**

Trudy: **Oh, yes. And I'm so excited. I love going to the zoo.**

Toby: **Well, where is Aunt Mary?**

Trudy: **She's not here yet. But I know she won't be long.**

Toby: **I'm not so sure. People don't always do what they say they will. The other day George said he would give me a bar of chocolate if I took my pet mouse to school and let it loose in the class room.**

Trudy: **Toby, you didn't do it?**

Toby: **Yes, I did.**

Trudy: **What happened?**

Toby: **Miss was ever so cross. I got a detention.**

Trudy: **At least you got the chocolate.**

Toby: **No, I didn't! George didn't keep his promise.**

Trudy: **Well, Aunt Mary is not like George. She'll keep her promise.**

Toby: **How do you know?**

Trudy: **She's a grown-up, and grown-ups always do what they say they will.**

Toby: **No they don't!**

Trudy: **Yes they do!**

Toby: **Dad doesn't.**

Trudy: **When didn't Dad do what he said?**

Toby: **Dad said he would take me to a football match last week if I kept my room tidy. And he didn't do it!**

Trudy: **But he couldn't, Toby. He was in bed with flu.**

Toby: **That's not the point. He told me he would do something and he didn't do it. And I did what he told me to. I kept my room tidy all week. Anyway, how do you know Aunt Mary isn't ill?**

Trudy: **She would have phoned Mum to tell her.**

Toby: **She could have forgotten, Trudy. People do forget, you know.**

Trudy: **Not Aunt Mary. She always does what she says she will.**

Toby: **I'm not so sure. I'm going home to get something to eat, then I think I might phone George and see if he wants to play football.**

Trudy: **Toby, you can't. Aunt Mary said we had to be ready to go as soon as she arrived. And she's coming here. If you're not ready you won't be able to go.**

Toby: **You can't always believe what people say, Trudy. I'm off. Don't hang around too long.**
Toby exits.

Trudy: **I do hope Toby is wrong. Aunt Mary has always done what she said before. But she is late. I do hope she comes soon.**
Trudy exits.

The leader comments on Trudy's dilemma. Should she do what Aunt Mary said? Why? *[Aunt Mary has always done what she said before.]*

ABOUT SERVING GOD ONLY

Toby: **Hello, boys and girls. I've had a great day. At lunchtime we went to the games field and played football. George came too. And I scored a great goal. In fact, I scored** 20 **goals. My team won by miles. I must be the best footballer in my school. I'd better find Trudy and tell her. Have you seen her anywhere? I'll just go and look.**

Toby disappears.

Toby: [off stage.] **Trudy! Trudy! Where are you?** *Toby reappears.*

Toby: **I can't find her anywhere. Girls! They're never around when you want them.** [*Calls*] **Trudy! Where are you? Can you help me call her? Say - 'Trudy! Where are you?' On the count of three. One, two, three. Trudy! Where are you?**

Trudy enters.

Trudy: **Was someone calling my name?**

Toby: **Yes, we all were.**

Trudy: **Well, what do you want? I hope it's important. I was busy doing my homework.**

Toby: **Don't worry about homework. I've got something much more important to tell you.**

Trudy: **What do you mean, don't worry about homework? If I don't do it I'll get into trouble. Mr Blenkinsop said if we don't give our homework in tomorrow we'll get a detention.**

Toby: **Oh bother Mr Blenkinsop. I've got much more important things to do than listen to him. Do you know, Trudy? I scored 20 goals today!**

Trudy: **Bet you didn't!**

Toby: **Yes I did. Well, I must have scored 15.**

Trudy: **Toby?**

Toby: **Well, 10 then.**

Trudy: **Honestly, Toby, you do tell lies. I'm going back to finish my homework. And you ought to do yours too.**

Toby: **No, listen, Trudy. Mike has got some new roller blades and I'm going roller blading with him. They're really fast - they have the super-fast wheels. It'll be really great!**

Trudy: **But what about your homework? You know what Mr Blenkinsop said.**

Toby: **Silly old teacher! I don't care what he said. I'm going roller blading.**

Trudy: **Where are your pads and helmet? You know Dad said you have to wear pads and a helmet when go roller blading.**

Toby: **I don't need pads. Or a helmet. They make me look like a sissy.**

Trudy: **Dad says, if you fall over without pads on you could really hurt yourself.**

Toby: **Bother Dad! He doesn't roller blade. What does he know about it? Anyway, I'm not going to fall over.**

Trudy: **Your trouble, Toby, is you never listen. You always think you know best.**

Toby: **Oh, phooey!** *Toby exits.*

Trudy: **Toby never listens when people tell him things. It's no wonder he's always getting into trouble. I hope he's all right. He really should have worn his pads and helmet.**

Loud noise of crashing.

Trudy: **I hope that wasn't Toby.** *Dashes off, calling:* **Toby! Toby! Are you all right?**

Trudy: [***Reappearing***] **It was Toby. He's fallen over and hit his head. They're taking him to hospital. I do hope it's nothing serious. Why didn't he listen to Dad?**

Lesson 37

GOD FORGIVES SIN

Leader: **Is everyone here who should be here? Stand up if you are not here. Where is Toby?**
Repeat but louder. Toby appears. Give a brief history of who Toby is and how long you have known him.

Leader: **Toby you also have a very good friend, don't you?**

Toby: **Nope!!**

Leader: **You little trickster you. You know whom I mean!**

Toby: **Nope!! No idea.**

Leader: **Now Toby! That special friend. You know, the one with the golden hair.**

Toby: **Don't you mean tarantula - that poisonous, 8-legged, man-eating spider?**

Leader: [indignantly] **Toby, that was a very unkind thing to say!**

Toby: **Well, Soooorrrreee.** [stretch the words out and emphasise the last syllable]

Leader: **We'll let the boys and girls decide. Trudy, please come out.**
Trudy appears shyly, bit by bit. She retreats once or twice.

Leader: **Boys let me introduce cool Trudy.**

Trudy: [confidently] **Hello goys and birls.**
Audience responds – ***hullo Trudy***

Toby: [looks down towards Trudy's feet] **What's that on your foot?**

Trudy: **Nothing.**

Toby: **What do you mean, nothing. Let me see.**
Toby disappears behind the screen.

Toby: [from behind the screen] **You've got your foot caught in a trap!**

Trudy: **Will you help me take it off?**
Toby reappears.

Toby: **I'm not sure .....**

Trudy: **Oh, thank you, thank you.**

Toby: **Hang on! I have a question to ask you.**

Trudy: [breaking in] **Toby, thank you, thank you - you've saved my life.**

Toby: **Trudy, I said I have something to ask you.**

Trudy: **Toby, I don't want you to ask me a question! Just help me get out of this trap.**

Toby: **Trudy, why are you caught in that trap?**

Trudy: **Toby, I said I didn't want you to ask me a question!**

Toby: **Trudy, would you please answer my question.**

Trudy: [getting uncomfortable] **I didn't mean to do it, Toby, honestly.**

Toby: **What didn't you mean to do?**

Trudy: **Get caught in that trap. Oh, Toby, it was awful, just awful!**

Toby: **Trudy, I'm going to ask you one more time, why are you caught in that trap?**

Trudy: [pauses and hems and haws for a bit] **Promise you won't be angry, Toby?**

Toby: **O.K. I promise.**

Trudy: **Well, I was just going to taste the grapes in the greenhouse - oh, Toby, they look so good and delicious and tasty, and then when ...**

Toby: **Trudy! Dad told us to stay away from the greenhouse ....**

Trudy: **But Toby, those grapes looked so delicious and so much nicer than the ones in the kitchen, I just had to try one. Then I heard Dad coming so I had to escape. I was so scared that I didn't look where I was going and I ran into this trap.**

Toby: **Trudy, do you know what the Bible says about that?**

Trudy: **About being caught in a trap?**

Toby: **No, Trudy, about giving into temptation. The Bible says when we give into temptation we get into trouble.**

Trudy: **Well, I'm in trouble, aren't I?**

Toby: **Yes, you are. And the only way you will get out of that trap is to find Dad and ask him to take it off.**

Trudy: **I can't!**

Toby: **Yes you can. Come on, I'll come with you.**
Toby and Trudy disappear.

Contents (in Bible Order)

Contents (in OTW for 3-9s order)

Subject Index

Christian Focus Publications publishes biblically-accurate books for adults and children.

If you are looking for quality Bible teaching for children then we have a wide and excellent range of Bible story books - from board books to teenage fiction, we have it covered.

You can also try our new Bible teaching Syllabus for 3-9 year olds and teaching materials for pre-school children.

These children's books are bright, fun and full of biblical truth, an ideal way to help children discover Jesus Christ for themselves. Our aim is to help children find out about God and get them enthusiastic about reading the Bible, now and later in their lives.

Find us at our web page: www.christianfocus.com

TnT

TnT Ministries (which stands for Teaching and Training Ministries) was launched in February 1993 by Christians from a broad variety of denominational backgrounds who are concerned that teaching the Bible to children be taken seriously. The leaders were in charge of a Sunday School of 50 teachers at St Helen's Bishopgate, an evangelical church in the city of London, for 13 years, during which time a range of Biblical teaching material has been developed. TnT Ministries also runs training days for Sunday School teachers.